DISCARD

A SUMMONS UNTO MEN

**AN ANTHOLOGY OF THE WRITINGS
OF JOHN HAYNES HOLMES**

EDITED, WITH FOREWORD, BY
CARL HERMANN VOSS

PREFACE BY
JAMES LUTHER ADAMS
DANA MacLEAN GREELEY
DONALD SZANTHO HARRINGTON

SIMON AND SCHUSTER : NEW YORK

PERMISSIONS

The editor and Simon and Schuster wish to thank the following authors, publishers and agents for permission to quote from the books and publications listed. All possible care has been taken to ensure accuracy, to trace the ownership of each selection included and to make full acknowledgment for its use. If, however, any errors have accidentally occurred, they will be corrected in subsequent editions, provided that notification is sent to the publisher.

AMERICAN JEWISH CONGRESS, New York: "The Man and His Works [Stephen S. Wise]" by John Haynes Holmes, from *Congress Weekly*, March 21, 1949, Vol. 16, No. 12, pp. 7–9.

BEACON PRESS, Boston: "A Modern Faith," from *The Beacon Song and Service Book*, copyright 1935 by Beacon Press, Inc., p. 72; *The Pilots* edited by Samuel A. Eliot, from *Heralds of a Liberal Faith*, Vol. IV, copyright 1952 by Beacon Press, pp. 7–8, 17; *The Personal Letters of Stephen Wise*, copyright © 1956 by Justine Wise Polier and James Waterman Wise, pp. 7–12. Reprinted by permission of Beacon Press.

THE BOBBS-MERRILL COMPANY, INC., Indianapolis: condensed from *Mysticism and the Modern Mind* edited by Alfred P. Stiernotte, copyright © 1959 by The Liberal Arts Press, Inc. Reprinted by permission of The Liberal Arts Press Division of The Bobbs-Merrill Company, Inc.

DODD, MEAD AND COMPANY, New York: *The Life and Letters of Robert Collyer* by John Haynes Holmes, copyright 1917, Vol. II, pp. 329–330; *The Grail of Life* edited by John Haynes Holmes and others, copyright 1919; *New Churches for Old*, copyright 1922; a poem, "A Tribute to John Haynes Holmes," by Angela Morgan, copyright 1926.

(Continued on page 244)

To *the Grandchildren
and Great-Grandchildren
of John Haynes Holmes*

ACKNOWLEDGMENTS

I am indebted to the libraries of the Meadville Theological School, the University of Chicago, Union Theological Seminary (New York City), Skidmore College, and the New York State Department of Education at Albany; the New York City Public Library; the Saratoga Springs Public Library; the Crandall Library, Glens Falls, New York; the Jacksonville Main Public Library, Jacksonville, Florida; and the Library of Congress, Washington, D. C., for research facilities and resources.

I wish to thank the trustees of the Arthur W. Schmidt Foundation for grants-in-aid in 1966–67 and 1968–69 for travel and research, transcribing and composition. I am grateful to three loyal supporters of my work for many years, the late H. J. Sobiloff, Myer Sobiloff, and Rudolph G. Sonneborn, as well as Mrs. James Boyd and the trustees of The Community Church of New York, for making possible the publication of this book.

To my friends Russell Henry Stafford and Sheldon Steinberg I am indebted for time and thought generously given in assistance with the assembling and revising of the manuscript, and James Luther Adams and Myles Martel for critical analyses of the Foreword.

To my wife, Phyllis Gierlotka Voss, I owe much for constant help, ranging from sensible counsel to domestic felicity.

This anthology of the writings of John Haynes Holmes is published with the permission and cooperation of his son and daughter, Roger Wellington Holmes and Frances Holmes Brown.

C. H. V.

CONTENTS

PREFACE

To our generation John Haynes Holmes was one of the foremost liberal ministers in America. In the ministry of liberal religion he had rivals, and among both evangelical Protestants and non-Christian religionists many men possessed power and skills comparable to his; but few were his peers in eloquence and effectiveness as writer and preacher. We, as Unitarian Universalists, attest to his eminence; and we honor his place in a noble tradition.

We know, however, that he belongs to others as well: to members of the Ethical Culture Society who recall his high regard for Felix Adler, his close cooperation with John Lovejoy Elliott in many civic causes; but also to Jews of every persuasion—Orthodox and Conservative, Reform and non-observant—who remember his unique understanding of Jewish thought and customs, his veneration of Judaism as an historic, living faith, his sensitivity to the religious ideals and values of such secular-minded Jews as Albert Einstein, Sigmund Freud, and Louis Brandeis, his early, informed espousal of Zionism, and, most noble of all, his defense of Jewry during the Hitler nightmare. Yet he is revered to this hour by many traditionally inclined Christians who know how insightful and devastating were his critiques of Christendom for its pretensions and inadequacies, but who are nonetheless inclined to describe Holmes's spirit and outlook as, in their words, "Christlike." In the National Association for the Advancement of Colored People and the American Civil Liberties Union, the International Fellowship of Reconciliation and the War Resisters' League, he had been both a founder and a leader. To all these groups he belongs—not merely to the Unitarian Universalist fellowship.

True, he decided in the dark days of World War I that, as a pacifist, he must disassociate himself from his fellow Unitarians, who almost to a man supported the war; but never could he break loose from the uniting bonds of friendship and kinship, especially among those who admired him and sought to emulate him. Frederick May Eliot understood this: as president of the American Unitarian Association, Eliot presented to Holmes in 1954 the Sixth Annual Unitarian Award for Distinguished Service to the Cause of Liberal Religion, saying, "You may no longer claim to belong to us, John; but you cannot forbid us to say that we belong with you." These words presaged a return, for, only a few years later, Holmes resumed his membership in the Unitarian Ministerial Association from which he had withdrawn almost four decades earlier.

We are grateful to Carl Hermann Voss for this memorial to the heritage of John Haynes Holmes, for encouraging a contemporary interest in the Holmes legacy, for placing him with accuracy and logic in the historic succession of William Ellery Channing and Theodore Parker, and for portraying him as an integral figure in the Social Gospel movement of American Protestantism. Dr. Voss has devoted many years to this subject, initially in the preparation of his scholarly and fascinating duo-biography, *Rabbi and Minister: The Friendship of Stephen S. Wise and John Haynes Holmes* (much of it in personal interviews in the 1950s and early 1960s with Holmes himself, who died on the very eve of that book's publication) and then in the careful research from which he has made this judicious selection for *A Summons unto Men: An Anthology of the Writings of John Haynes Holmes*. Since the inception of *A Summons unto Men* we have encouraged its editor, and with keen interest we have followed its development. He has justified our faith in him and his project.

We welcome the emergence of this book, give it our whole-hearted approval, and hope it will reach a wide audience, so that men and women in years to come may perceive how significant John Haynes Holmes was in the first half of the twentieth century. Dr. Holmes brought, by precept and example, the spiritual heritage of a host of great men and women into the lives of untold numbers of people. We keep this influence alive by making his words available anew for an age standing in need of him.

JAMES LUTHER ADAMS
DANA MACLEAN GREELEY
DONALD SZANTHO HARRINGTON

FOREWORD

In 1907 the young John Haynes Holmes came from Dorchester, Massachusetts, to the Church of the Messiah (Unitarian) in New York City and set in motion events that altered the name and program of that famous church but also broadened horizons and set new goals for the American Unitarian Association. The Community Church of New York and the Unitarian Universalist Association owe to him much of their creative force today.

In those early days of his ministry, Holmes still had hope for the Christian Church, because he believed there was no other movement in human history which could be compared with Christianity as a civilizing influence. In the years prior to the First World War, Holmes expected Christianity to rise to a new level of influence and power and anticipated a new theology to replace the old, which had, he felt, been retrogressive and nonrational. He was in accord with Walter Rauschenbusch of Rochester, New York, famed exponent of the Social Gospel, in claiming that the new social thrust of the churches was realizing the purpose of Christianity. His faith was grounded in a God more immanent than transcendent, and he counted himself among those who believed in the Divine within man, God with Whom men were co-workers.

He relied upon the meditative aspects of religion solely for strength and courage to venture forth in quest of justice in an unjust world. Yet in wistful musing near life's end, he recalled the Church of the Messiah in his autobiography, *I Speak for Myself* (page 99), as "a noble structure, dark, dignified, and beautiful. I loved to adorn it, and had special services of prayer and praise, with emphasis on worship as contrasted with preaching. It was through the quiet uplift of this church that I found myself to be a mystic, with inward powers of the spirit I was neglecting. I have often wondered where I might have been led had I given these powers release." Some of those powers found expression in the powerful hymns he wrote, many of which are included in most Protestant hymnals of the present.

He believed in a "spiritual Christianity"; but he went beyond the bounds of Christianity and, like most Unitarians of that time, did not interpret Jesus as the Divine Christ, the very Son of God, a transempirical event, the Center of History, who revealed the ultimate meaning of life and illustrated supremely the Divine Initiative. Focusing on the historical Jesus, he adjudged "Saviorship" to be an obsolete theological term and interpreted Jesus as a revolutionary who sought to bring love in all its potency. Holmes looked upon the Bible not as the core of his faith nor as an indispensable source of dogma but rather as splendid literature and fascinating history. He knew the Bible thoroughly, loved it for its lore and legends, and used it in an illustrative way. He considered the Old Testament and the New to be supreme examples of moral poetry.

Indebted to William Ellery Channing, founder of the Unitarian movement in North America, for liberating ideas and inspiration, he acknowledged an even greater intellectual and spiritual debt to Theodore Parker, the famous abolitionist, who was his ideal and exemplar. In Holmes's estimation, Parker's work during his brief career of the pre–Civil War era marked him as the foremost religious leader America had produced. Channing and Parker were, however, only two of many formative influences.

Asked who his father's mentors had been, Roger Wellington Holmes, professor of philosophy at Mount Holyoke College, responded:

Father had few "mentors" in the usual sense: they would have been uncharacteristic of him. Rather he had preceptors. Large among Father's preceptors were the great English poets and dramatists from Shakespeare to Alexander Pope and Tennyson to George Bernard Shaw. Sir Walter Scott was his hero.

He was an omnivorous reader of English poetry: on his trip to India in 1947, this was the chief reading he took with him. He read very widely in English and American literature; but the men he read were moralists, like Emerson. I can remember his saying that a great play must have a great moral. He would have said the same of poetry in general. In all of this he was a Platonist: all Truth and all Beauty have to be Good.

Father's chief "mentor" was Herbert Spencer. As a believer in evolution he was more Spencerian than Darwinian. It was Darwin's empirical approach to metaphysics rather than his specific evolutionary theory that excited Father; but in a modern or complete sense he was not Darwinian at all, for he was much more impressed and moved by the creative evolution of Henri Bergson and its religious implications.

In brief, Father could be said to have been a nineteenth-century Protestant liberal. He did not read much theology after leaving Harvard; I do not think he was interested in theological controversy. Like most liberals of his type, he thought theology sterile.

Father had many preceptors, however, before the nineteenth century. Prominent among them were Socrates and Plato; and he often read the great Romans like Cicero, Seneca, and Marcus Aurelius. The Rome of the great orators was closer to his heart than Athens. Then there is a real gap. He seemed to have been unmoved by even the best of the Middle Ages.

If we can call Shakespeare a "preceptor," it could be said that Shakespeare was Father's foremost pre-nineteenth-century preceptor. He knew Shakespeare's great moral plays by heart:

Hamlet, King Lear, Macbeth, The Merchant of Venice, Julius Caesar, Richard the Second, Coriolanus, Othello, etc.

The roots of the nineteenth century he loved so much were in the eighteenth-century Enlightenment, and he was well acquainted with the Enlightenment. Kantian ethics he knew particularly well, and it had a strong influence on him.

Typical of nineteenth-century liberals, he was not a supernaturalist. When Father and I talked about such things I had the distinct impression that his only articles of faith were his belief in personal immortality and in the moral order of the universe. He was firmly with Theodore Parker in the conviction that while the arc of the universe is long, it bends toward righteousness. Indeed, it was this sense of morality that was his greatness. He seemed to have a special understanding of the moral forces at work—and not at work—in his world; and within him there was a tremendous moral drive that took practically all of his energy and his time.

Dr. Roger W. Holmes assesses his father accurately when he depicts him as a man bent on achieving morality in society and justice for all mankind. To these objectives John Haynes Holmes gave himself without stint into his ninth decade. Until his death in his eighty-fourth year, he was outraged by "man's inhumanity to man"; and until his dying day he trusted that men might move ever nearer the goal of his fellow Social Gospelers, namely, "the Kingdom of God on earth."

John Haynes Holmes's special concerns were the welfare of the blacks in the United States, the freeing of the people of India, and the defense of Jews against the attacks of anti-Semites. He had the fearlessness of a man who, while not coveting martyrdom, stood ready to die for principle if need be; he proved it by preaching on controversial issues and airing unorthodox, unpopular views. High on the list of such courageous opinions was Holmes's conviction that the capitalist system was responsible for the poverty of men and the ever-mounting cruelty and inhumanity in the world; that the chief business of the church was to hasten the day when the profit-seeking economy of the modern era would give way to a socialist society.

This Christian Socialism, as it was then known, characterized Holmes's preaching and writing in the first decades of the twentieth century. Signs of intense social consciousness were visible in Dorchester during his first pastorate of 1904–07; but his anticapitalist views, becoming more pronounced in subsequent years, came vividly to the fore when he befriended Eugene V. Debs during the Socialist leader's imprisonment at the close of World War I. Holmes joined the Socialist Party, but refused to submit to Party discipline, characteristically rejecting any control over his utterances as a socialist. He sought to ally himself with any organization or movement bent on alleviating social imbalances and ameliorating the ills of a patently unjust society. After Debs's withdrawal from the national scene, Holmes joined the supporters of Robert La Follette's short-lived Progressive Party in the 1924 presidential campaign; but he supported the Socialist Party candidates in 1928, through the thirties and the forties, preferring the views and objectives of a Norman Thomas to those of an Alfred E. Smith, a Franklin D. Roosevelt, or a Harry S. Truman.

To utter these viewpoints he needed and created for himself a free pulpit. The principle of freedom of the pulpit for which he stood became an incomparable legacy not only for his colleagues and successors on whose behalf the church trustees continuously affirmed their ministers' right to speak without censorship or restraint, but for future generations in the ministry at large.

By 1918–19 Holmes had chosen for himself the status of an "Independent" and transformed the Church of the Messiah into the Community Church. His congregation encouraged him to broaden the program, enlarge the membership on as broad a basis as possible, and enter the post–World War I years with the intention of making a direct impact on society not only in New York City, but in national and international life as well; they agreed with Holmes about the importance of voluntary associations to implement a religious vision and seek fulfillment of the democratic ideal.

His Community Church of New York City set a standard throughout the country for other community churches. Most of them became interfaith, but few were interracial. Holmes's 1919 charge to his people, in his widely circulated sermon "What Is a Community Church?," for a "universal, humanistic religion which knows no bounds of any kind, not even Christianity, . . . eliminating every last vestige of theology . . . [and] thus relegating all matters of belief to private individual opinion," was not fulfilled, for he could not wipe out theological speculation and thought.

Yet he had some reward: he placed before the congregation the ideal of "membership and institution on an out-and-out citizenship basis, welcoming to our church any person who is part of our great American community, be he rich or poor, black or white, Christian, Jew, Hindu, or Parsee." This latter objective they did attain. Under the aegis of the church he served, as well as in the many books and hymns he wrote and in the pages of the magazine *Unity* he edited, he dealt with specific problems of social justice and international conflict. His greatest contributions toward these ends were the time and effort he devoted to the National Association for the Advancement of Colored People and the American Civil Liberties Union; of both organizations he was a founder and an officer from their inception in 1909 and 1920, respectively, until the end of his life.

Few of Holmes's friends and associates in the liberal and radical movements of the time shared his love for the church or his belief in its power to change and become a powerful

agent for progress. These men and women disappointed him
when they failed to give active support to the Community
Church in New York City; yet instead of resenting their de-
tachment, he persisted in construing their secular labors as
religious in motivation and results. Of such friends he had many.

Foremost among Holmes's friendships were those with Rabbi
Stephen S. Wise and Mahatma Gandhi, who shared his hopes
and aspirations. During their more than four decades in New
York (1907–49) Wise and Holmes were the closest of friends,
confidants in personal matters and pioneers in interfaith cooperation; though differing with Wise on war and peace, Holmes was
at one with him on issues ranging from Zionism to civic affairs.
In Gandhi Holmes found a true blending of East and West; in
1958, ten years after Gandhi's assassination, Holmes wrote to
me: "The greatest thing that has happened since Gandhi's
death is the work of Martin Luther King, who has taken the
whole law and gospel of Gandhi's teaching and proved its
worth anew."

Holmes had critics too. Many claimed he used the Community Church only as a sounding board for his views rather
than as a pastoral post. They overlooked the outreach of his
ministerial work, which was reflected in his fidelity as a pastor,
in his personal counseling and especially in his ministry of the
mails, for he maintained a vast correspondence through more
than half a century for troubled persons who wrote to him for
guidance and discovered that the inordinately busy Holmes
never lacked time to respond with letters of comfort and advice.
Some critical minds considered his sermons and articles flam-
boyant and polemical and found him merciless in attacks on
positions other than his own; they accused him of overdramatiz-
ing incidents, centering his preachments around himself, offering easy solutions for the intricate problems of a complex
society, and giving religious answers inadequate for twentieth-
century issues. His defenders, however, welcomed occasional

extremes as natural expressions of his temperament and justifiable means for laudable ends; they claimed he had a certain hyperbole of expression because he expressed his thought exactly as he felt it, and they considered him a powerful antidote to the poisons of false religion, finding him extraordinarily effective in denouncing wrong.

There were, indeed, weaknesses in Holmes's beliefs and actions, as even his champions admitted. He had a simplistic approach to problems both individual and social and was often naïve about men's motives, seemingly unaware of the extent of evil in the world and confident that moral suasion would alter an inequitable society. His enthusiasm often outstripped the realism that experience might have dictated; he allowed judgments to be colored by personal relationships with people who did not deserve such trust, and on occasion his endorsement of causes and individuals was excessive. He considered democracy to be the ultimate in political development and the essence of high religion and was convinced that man could depend on science to create a better world. He underestimated the class struggle and retained illusions about the possibility of dislodging deeply entrenched interests of power. He seemed unaware of the collective egoism of social organisms and appeared not to discern the close tie between conduct and interest in both individual and society.

Behind and beneath all this work, however, was a profoundly religious spirit. Freely admitting that his was a "humanistic interpretation of religion," Holmes adhered nevertheless to theism, for belief in God was to him inescapable: "In man is the highest expression of the Godhead, and in the exaltation of man the all-sufficient revelation of the Most High." He related his religious convictions directly to the most pressing problems of his day and had a keen awareness of contemporary trends, as well as a prescience of things to come. Long before it became fashionable to do so, Holmes had warned of the secularization of society, deplored the unrelatedness of organized religion, damned the inequities of mercantile capitalism, condemned war, denounced anti-Semitism, demanded equal rights and power for blacks.

I am grateful for having known the man for thirty-five years of his life, for having worked with him in many causes, and for having had the blessing of his friendship. For all these gifts— his life and work, his mind and spirit—I, like many others, am truly thankful.

CARL HERMANN VOSS

Spring, 1971
Jacksonville, Florida

CHRONOLOGY:

JOHN HAYNES HOLMES

1879   Born November 29, Philadelphia.

1894   Graduated grammar school, Malden, Massachusetts.

1898   Graduated Malden High School. Entered Harvard College.

1899   Began teaching in Sunday school of the Unitarian Church, Cambridge, Massachusetts.

1900   Became Sunday-school superintendent of Cambridge church.

1901   Entered Harvard Divinity School. Elected to Phi Beta Kappa.

1902   Graduated Harvard College, with degree of Bachelor of Arts, *summa cum laude.* Became student minister, Unitarian church, Danvers, Massachusetts.

1904   Installed March 2 as minister of Third Religious Society and Third Congregational Church (Unitarian) of Dorchester, Massachusetts. Married Madeleine Hosmer Baker, June 27, in Church of the Saviour, Brooklyn, New York. Graduated Divinity School, Harvard University, with degree of Bachelor of Divinity.

1905   Birth of son, Roger Wellington Holmes.

1906   Published first book, collection of sermons, *The Old and The New.*

1907   Began ministry in Church of the Messiah, New York City, February 3.

1908   Birth of daughter, Frances Adria Holmes. Helped found Unitarian Fellowship for Social Justice. Lectured at newly organized Ford Hall Forum in Boston, first of annual appearances in following four decades.

1909   Served as one of five incorporators of National Association for the Advancement of Colored People, February 12 (Lincoln's 100th birthday).

1910   Appointed associate editor of *Unity* (edited by Jenkin Lloyd Jones) and contributing editor of *The Unitarian Advance* (a new department, "The Modern Church"). Joined Stephen S. Wise and Frank Oliver Hall in nonsectarian union services of Free Synagogue, Universalist Church of the Divine Paternity, and Church of the Messiah on general subject "Religion and the Social Problem."

1911   With Stephen S. Wise, led public protest against industrial abuses which caused tragic Triangle Shirtwaist Company fire in New York City.

1912   Published *The Revolutionary Function of the Modern Church*. Supported Theodore Roosevelt for U. S. Presidency. Officiated at funeral of predecessor, Robert Collyer (b. 1823).

1913   Visited British Isles for first time. Wrote hymn, "The Voice of God Is Calling." Published *Clear Grit*, collection of Robert Collyer's unpublished poems and addresses, and his own newest book, *Marriage and Divorce*.

1914   Reaffirmed pacifist stand as Great War began in August. Wrote special hymn for nationwide observance of President's Peace Day in October.

1915   Joined with John R. Mott, Leyton Richards and Richard Roberts in founding American branch of International Fellowship of Reconciliation. Published *Is Death the End?*

1916   Helped found the American Union Against Militarism and its National Civil Liberties Bureau, later to become the American Civil Liberties Union. Published *New Wars for Old*.

1917   In "A Statement to My People on the Eve of War"

asserted stand of absolute pacifism; supported by church trustees despite their nonpacifism. Began series of annual union Thanksgiving services of Free Synagogue and Church of the Messiah. Published *Religion for Today* and *The Life and Letters of Robert Collyer.*

1918 Became editor of *Unity* and contributing editor of *The World Tomorrow.* Declined invitation to succeed late Jenkin Lloyd Jones at Abraham Lincoln Center in Chicago. Published anthology, *Readings from Great Authors.*

1919 Led congregation in transition from Church of the Messiah to The Community Church of New York. Fire destroyed church structure, September 11. Published anthology on immortality, *The Grail of Life.* Became co-editor (with Francis Nielson) of *Unity.*

1920 Continued Community Church services in New Amsterdam Theatre and the Community Forum on Sunday evenings in auditorium of Ethical Culture Society. With Clarence R. Skinner of Tufts University, founded the Community Church of Boston. Led Joint Steel Strikers' Aid Committee. Joined Harry F. Ward and Roger Baldwin in organizing American Civil Liberties Union. Published *Is Violence the Way Out?*

1921 Preached on subject "Who Is the Greatest Man in the World Today?," thus introducing Mahatma Gandhi to the American public.

1922 Traveled on European Continent and in Soviet Russia. Published *New Churches for Old.*

1923 Taught course on "Aspects of Christian Worship and Preaching" at newly founded Jewish Institute of Religion (Stephen S. Wise, founder and acting president). Held services for next 20 years in Town Hall.

1924 Campaigned on behalf of Robert La Follette, candidate of Progressive Party for U. S. Presidency.

1925 Observed centennial of The Community Church of New

York (formerly Church of the Messiah). Published *Patriotism Is Not Enough*.

1926 Took part in Passaic textile strike. Became editor in chief of *Unity*.

1927 Led in defense of Sacco and Vanzetti.

1928 Gave leadership in campaign for Outlawry of War Pact, in cooperation with Chicago lawyer Salmon O. Levinson, founder of the movement. Supported Norman Thomas, Socialist Party candidate for U. S. Presidency.

1929 Traveled to Middle East in January–February, accompanied by Mrs. Holmes and son Roger. In late autumn, published *Palestine: Today and Tomorrow*.

1930 Received Doctor of Divinity degree from Jewish Institute of Religion. Organized, with Stephen S. Wise, City Affairs Committee to uncover corruption in New York City politics and to seek ouster of Mayor James J. Walker (who resigned in September, 1932). Founded Mental Hygiene Consultation Service at The Community Church, assisted by Dr. Alfred Adler and Dr. Beran Wolfe, one of the first such centers in the United States.

1931 Continued with even more active program of City Affairs Committee, pressing Governor Franklin Delano Roosevelt for action against Tammany Hall. Received Doctor of Divinity degree from St. Lawrence University. Accompanied Sherwood Eddy's seminar to Europe and Soviet Union. Met Mahatma Gandhi in London. Became contributing editor of *Opinion: A Journal of Jewish Life and Letters* (James Waterman Wise and Stephen S. Wise founders and editors), writing regular column, "Through Gentile Eyes."

1932 Celebrated 25th anniversary of ministry in New York City. Published two new books, *The Sensible Man's View of Religion*, a book of sermons with introduction by Stephen S. Wise, and *The Heart of Scott's Poetry*.

1933 Aided Stephen S. Wise in anti-Hitler protests. Wrote initial drafts of an antiwar play. Aided Drs. Hannah and Abraham Stone in founding Marriage Consultation Service at Community Church, first of its kind in U. S.

1935 Visited the Third Reich of Nazi Germany, returning with apprehension for fate of European Jews. Theatre Guild produced play, *If This Be Treason*, published in book form later in year (Reginald Lawrence, co-author).

1938 Accompanied by daughter Frances, took European journey. Published *Through Gentile Eyes*, a collection of articles from *Opinion*, and *Rethinking Religion*, a series of WQXR radio talks.

1939 Reaffirmed pacifist stand in *Christian Century* series, "If America Enters the War, What Shall I Do?"

1940 Elected chairman of American Civil Liberties Union. Laid cornerstone of new church on East Thirty-fifth Street between Park and Madison Avenues.

1941 On Sunday after Pearl Harbor, presented resignation to trustees of Community Church; resignation rejected on following day. Freedom of pulpit reaffirmed and his right to pacifist views established anew.

1942 Published *Out of Darkness*, dedicated to "My Beloved Comrades in the Fellowship of Reconciliation."

1943 Published *The Second Christmas and Other Stories*.

1944 Installed Donald Harrington of Chicago as junior colleague.

1945 Awarded Doctor of Divinity degree by Meadville Theological School at University of Chicago. Relinquished position as editor in chief of *Unity*.

1946 Gave Ingersoll Lecture on Immortality at Harvard University.

1947 Published *The Affirmation of Immortality* (Ingersoll Lecture). Accompanied by son Roger, visited India as lecturer on Watumull Foundation. Received Doctor of Letters degree at University of Benares. Saw Gandhi for last time, three months before Gandhi's assassination.

1948 Dedicated new edifice of The Community Church. Learned he had Parkinson's disease and decided to retire in February, 1949, on 42nd anniversary of his coming to New York.

1949 Installed Donald Harrington as senior minister of The Community Church on March 28.

1950 Retired as chairman of American Civil Liberties Union.

1951 Received Doctor of Divinity degree from Rollins College.

1952 Helped to dedicate The John Haynes Holmes Community House adjacent to The Community Church.

1953 Published *My Gandhi.*

1956 Ordained grandson, David Wellington Brown, to Unitarian ministry.

1958 Published autobiography, *I Speak for Myself.*

1960 Published *The Collected Hymns of John Haynes Holmes.*

1961 Death of wife, Madeleine Baker Holmes, May 28.

1964 Died, April 3.

The voice of God is calling
    Its summons unto men;
As once he spake in Zion,
    So now he speaks again:
Whom shall I send to succor
    My people in their need,
Whom shall I send to loosen
    The bonds of shame and greed? . . .
                    —J. H. H., 1913

I

THE MINISTER
AND PUBLIC FIGURE

Like a swimmer charting course
  From the mouth of some great stream
To the highlands of its source
  Must the saint pursue his dream.
Set against the mighty sweep
  Of the water's downward flow,
He a tryst with God must keep
  On the summit's feeding snow.

> —MARY CRAIG SINCLAIR,
> "The Saint," 1920,
> dedicated to J. H. H.

THE AGE OF CONFIDENCE

That was the golden after-glow of the nineteenth century, which itself outdid in splendor everything since the Periclean Age of classic Greece. Those of you who did not live in that period before 1914, or are not old enough to remember it, cannot imagine the security we enjoyed and the serenity we felt in that old world. Mankind had known nothing like it since the age of the Antonines, the happiest of ancient times. It was true that politics were corrupt, and big business oppressive, and poverty rife, but these were hangovers of a past out of which, as by a very law of progress, we were emerging into an ideally just and free society. It was true also that competitive armaments were heavy, diplomacy dishonest, and empires arrogant and cruel, but peace was on the way, and there would never be another war. Nothing could shake our equanimity. Confidence in human events was not less than confidence in the stars. We were fatalists in the sense that we believed that not the worst but the best was certain.

Sermon, "Forty Years of It!,"
The Community Pulpit, 1947

THE ABOLITIONIST HERITAGE

I awoke to life in a family bathed in the tradition of the anti-slavery struggle. At intervals, for a period of years during my youth, I sat at the feet of a great-uncle who wore the blue from Bull Run to Appomattox. The flame of freedom for the slaves still burned in his soul as when he fought at Gettysburg, and later marched from Atlanta to the sea. More constant and more important was the influence of my grandfather [John Cummings Haynes], who was an Abolitionist in the day of [William Lloyd] Garrison and [Wendell] Phillips, and one of the young men who resolved in 1850 "that Theodore Parker be given a chance to be heard in Boston." A hundred times, from the lips of this beloved man, I heard the story of the anti-slavery meetings, of the assault on [Charles] Sumner, of Anthony Burns, of John Brown and Harpers Ferry, of Theodore Parker and the Boston Music Hall. Through him I met some of the heroes of the great days—Thomas Wentworth Higginson, Frank Sanborn, Julia Ward Howe. In his library I read books, letters, documents—memorials of the battle for emancipation. Thus early was I grounded in an abiding sense of the rights of man, moved to pity for the downtrodden and oppressed, taught that only by labor, sacrifice and struggle can liberty be won. . . . [By reading the writings of Theodore Parker I] saw religion in militant action against the crowning social evil of its day and understood religion from this time on to be thus an heroic crusade in the name of God for the establishment of justice and brotherhood.

> Article, "What Is Worth Fighting for in American Life?," in *Survey*, February 1, 1927

MY FATHER

My father never had a chance, most men never have a chance, in those matters that pertain to the higher interests of life. I was given my chance, and took it. From that hour on I have felt dedicated to the task of using it for the liberation of those less fortunate than myself. . . .

If there is any one thing which I most like to recall in connection with my father, it is that he grew throughout his life. He was never old, even when his body was broken and his mind dim. He started with little education, and made his own way in the rich treasury of literature and of art. He worked himself free from the entanglements of orthodox Christianity, and followed on and on the adventurous highway of free thought. He was reared in the individualism of the nineteenth century, and in the last years welcomed the socialism of the twentieth century. He grew up enamored of all the familiar tradition of war, and died a convinced pacifist. He revered tradition and respected convention, but was always ready for a discovery of new truth and an experiment with new experience. He moved with the changes in the literature, philosophy, science, politics and religion of his time, and never found a stopping-place. From him I derived a momentum of the spirit which has carried me to this day, and which I trust may speed me ever to new goals.

Essay in symposium, *What I Owe to My Father*, 1931

AN ACCOUNT OF MY MINISTRY

My decision to enter the ministry as my life-work must have found its way into my subconscious, as we say in these psychoanalytic days, when I was a boy in high school, and became a definite resolve when I was in college. I think my family had a good deal to do with what happened. . . . I thought I should like to serve the church, and be a leader in its work. I was impressed by its dignity and solemnity, and was interested in the preaching. My father encouraged me, and, as I grew older, took me to some of the great churches of various denominations in Boston. Thus, I early became acquainted with religion in its wider and more general aspects, and liked it.

A second influence was that of Dr. Minot J. Savage, curiously enough my predecessor in this pulpit (1896–1906), and in my boyhood the highly popular and influential minister of the Church of the Unity in Boston. . . . Not infrequently it was my custom to spend a weekend in the big house with my grand-parents, and on such occasions they always took me with them on Sunday morning to hear Dr. Savage. Here I had my first intimate experience with crowded congregations and great preaching. I can remember thinking how wonderful it must be to preach like that, and to have such an audience to listen. . . . Sunday after Sunday, as I listened to Dr. Savage, I indulged myself in the audacious excitement of putting myself in his place. My homiletical training began at this preacher's feet. More than Dr. Savage ever realized, he made me a minister of religion, and therewith bred up his own successor.

But there was another and final influence which led me into the ministry. I refer to Theodore Parker, the great American preacher, who flourished a hundred years ago [d. 1860]. . . . I learned the heroic story of Parker's heresy and his long battle for spiritual freedom as a part of the history of my country. On my first visit to Europe, I made a sacred pilgrimage to Parker's grave in the city of Florence, where he died. I think it was Theodore Parker who taught me the real meaning of religion as an inward experience of God which expressed itself out-wardly not merely in prayer and praise, but in a passion for righteousness, and a ceaseless labor for the weak, helpless and downtrodden among men. I admired Parker's scholarship, his magnificent powers as a preacher, his courage in seeking and proclaiming truth, his demonstration of the effective idealism of religion. What stirred me was the way Parker lived his faith—especially his unsparing fight against chattel slavery and the evils of poverty. . . . It was to Parker's spirit that I cried, like Hamlet to his father's ghost, "Go on, I'll follow thee."

These were the influences that made me a minister. So it

was three years in [Harvard] College, three years in the Divinity School, three years in my first parish in Dorchester, Massachusetts! Then in November, 1906, I received the call to New York. I accepted this call, and on February 3, 1907, preached my first sermon in my new pulpit. . . .

When this twenty-seven-year-old minister looked into the faces of that first congregation, in 1907, he saw a group of persons of prevailingly conservative, even reactionary, ideas. For Unitarians of that far-off day were radical theologically, but not otherwise.

This same ironical fact was true also of myself. Believe it or not, I was a conservative. Thus I was opposed to woman suffrage. I was hostile to the popular election of senators. I had little or no use for trade unions. I applauded the famous remark of President Eliot, of Harvard, that the "scab" was the great American hero. I was reading Herbert Spencer, with warm endorsement of his philosophy of individualism. How all this is to be reconciled with my enthusiasm for Theodore Parker is more than I can say. I can only suggest that it was one more instance of that unconscious conflict between Puritan idealism and Puritan dogmatism which has always been more or less characteristic of New England.

Such a conflict, conscious or unconscious, was bound to end in some kind of an explosion, which was prepared, in my case, by my belated reading of such books as Henry George's *Progress and Poverty*, Henry Demarest Lloyd's *Wealth against Commonwealth*, Edward Bellamy's *Looking Backward*, and Walter Rauschenbusch's *Christianity and the Social Crisis*. Then I was excited by Washington Gladden's great controversy over "tainted money." The last straw, so to speak, came with my advent in New York, where I met with the leaders of radical opinion, and especially came under the influence of my beloved and mighty colleague, that great prophet of the spirit, Rabbi Stephen Wise.

All at once, to the vast consternation of my people, I became a tireless and, I fear, rather noisy social reformer. I began preaching sermons on socialism. I lifted my voice as an ardent advocate of labor. I made Eugene Victor Debs my friend, and when the McNamara brothers blew up the Los Angeles *Times* building, I ventured to speak a word in their defense [1911–12]. I attacked capitalism, not its evils merely, but its system. I was all for revolution—a peaceful revolution, to be sure, but one which would overturn society, in favor of a more righteous social order.

What really concerned me was the new interpretation of Christianity as a socialized religion. There was nothing particularly new or strange about this. It was all to be found in Theodore Parker. Indeed, it went back as far at least as Jesus and the Prophets, and the whole Jewish-Christian conception of the Kingdom. But it was new in our times, and shook the religious world to its foundations.

Those were exciting days in the old church—the young minister in his sudden enthusiasm all but blowing his head off, as though he were suddenly gone mad, and the congregation, at least the older members, looking as though they were hearing the explosion of an atomic bomb.

The Church of the Messiah, as it was then called, was a Unitarian church in the strictest and narrowest sense of the word. I fitted perfectly into the picture, as I had been born and bred a Unitarian, and was an ardent devotee of that faith. Indeed, I can still recall that I came on to New York with the high resolve to make this church the Cathedral Church of American Unitarianism. Here were the money, the location, the tradition. Why not? But very soon I seemed to note that the new people who began coming to the church were only exceptionally Unitarians. They represented a cross-section of a city, in which Unitarianism was only the merest fraction of the community. Should I be concerned only with this fraction, and ignore all the rest of the population? How could I justify a church which turned away from the vast majority of the people, and was thus content with a little group of highly selective persons? Why not take the situation as I found it in the city, and make my church an inclusive institution for all sorts and conditions of men? Why seek to impose a denominational interest, and thus divide men along lines of theological distinction of which now they were altogether unconscious? The mission of a church, after all, is to unite people, not divide them. Now, the community, which is the common life, unites, while the denomination, which is the sectarian interest, divides. Why not, therefore, a community instead of a Unitarian church?

A community church, dedicated to the services of those social and ethical ideals which must make humanity one in prosperity and peace, and in the assurance of brotherhood, upon this earth! It was a mighty transformation, wrought by struggle and sacrifice, and an unfaltering faith. Had he been able to look ahead and see, I doubt if the young minister would have dared to come here to New York on that fateful day in 1907. Nor do I believe the people would have wanted him to come. Those were days of quietness and confidence, and disturbance was unwelcome. . . .

The people of the Community Church of New York were, however, faithful to the ideal of freedom. . . . If there is anywhere a free pulpit in America, it is in the Community Church of New York.

This congregation encountered such disasters and suffered such losses as can scarcely be believed, in a single generation . . . passed through two unprecedented wars, and an economic depression of unparalleled proportions, . . . incredible misfortunes [that] began on that September day in 1919 when the Church of the Messiah was burned to the ground. In the . . . years which . . . passed since that catastrophe, [the congregation] . . .

built out of [its] own resources two new churches, and, in the intervals, spent eighteen years without a home—in Town Hall and other temporary camping grounds. . . . Losing everything [the congregation] . . . recovered everything—nay, more, . . . used disaster to make history in the construction of this edifice [40 East Thirty-fifth Street] as a monument of modernistic art. Where can be found a generosity to match [such] achievement, a sacrifice to equal [such] utter dedication? If ever a church belonged to its people, this church [does], . . . bought, . . . as Paul bought his Roman citizenship, "at a great price."

The brotherhood came true alike in worship and in work, . . . peoples of every nationality and race, of every color, creed and class. The daily practice of the Community Church is what men have dreamed of since the beginning of the world and still are dreaming. . . .

> Sermon, *The Community Pulpit,*
> 1949

THE PURPOSE OF THE COMMUNITY CHURCH

In quest of a definition which would hold, I wrought out a statement summarizing the distinctive characteristics of the Community Church which is as useful today as it was on the day it was composed. It runs as follows:

"The Community Church is an institution of religion dedicated to the service of humanity. It is distinctive from other churches in these points:

"It substitutes for loyalty to the single denomination, *loyalty to the social group.* Its first affiliation is not with any denomination, but with the community as a whole.

"It substitutes for a private group of persons held together by common theological beliefs or viewpoints, *the public group of citizens held together by common social interests.* It excludes none but welcomes all, regardless of sect, class, nation or race, on a basis of membership identical with that of citizenship in the community.

"It substitutes for restrictions of creed, ritual, or ecclesiastical organization, *the free spirit.* It relegates all matters of theology and worship where they belong—to the unfettered thought and conviction of the individual.

"It substitutes for the individual *the social group,* as an object of salvation. It interprets religion in terms of social reconstruction, and dedicates its members to the fulfillment of social idealism.

"It substitutes for Christianity as a religion of special revelation, *the idea of universal religion.* It regards the religious instinct as inherent in human nature, and all religions as contributions to the fulfillment of man's higher life.

"It substitutes for the theistic, *the humanistic* point of view; for absorption in the next world, *dedication to a better life in this world;* for the church as a sacred institution, *the idea of present society as fulfilling the 'Kingdom of God'—the commonwealth of man.*

"The Community Church is the practical acknowledgment of religion as the Spirit of Love incarnate in human fellowship. The core of its faith, as the purpose of its life, is *'the Beloved Community.'* "

I Speak for Myself, 1958

ROBERT COLLYER
(1823–1912)

The relation of Holmes to Collyer was like that of a son to his father: profound respect and admiration characterized the young man's attitude toward the venerable minister who was fifty-six years his senior. Holmes appreciated most of all the unflinching fidelity of the old man to him, the junior minister of the Church of the Messiah, and he recalled the association with gratitude in his two-volume biography of 1917, The Life and Letters of Robert Collyer (Vol. II, pp. 329–30): ". . . When dear friends of the years gone by came to him and made complaint against the heresies of the new minister, he refused to listen, and told them, with such sharpness as he could command, that their duty was loyalty to the man they had chosen to lead."

In a later year one of the members gave Holmes a letter of December 31, 1910, in which Collyer had written: "We have a young man of burning enthusiasm touching Socialism. He gives it to us hot and hot, and has a fine hearing. The church is on the way again to prosperity."

The church lost an irreplaceable treasure near midnight of Saturday, November 30, 1912, when Robert Collyer died. The announcement made by Holmes in the church service was the first inkling many in the congregation had of the great loss they now suffered. Holmes's voice suddenly broke as he said, "Like Enoch in the Bible, of whom Dr. Collyer preached so often, he was not, for God took him."

So much of Robert Collyer was personality rather than learning, or public service, or statesmanship, or authorship, or even preaching, that his story must be anecdotal rather than historical. Yet it all hangs together in an integrity which was its own. For five years (1907–1912) Collyer and I abode in a spiritual unity of mind and heart [as senior and junior ministers of the Church of the Messiah]. There were fifty-six years between the older and the younger man. It would seem that this span of time would preclude all general understanding. But the bond between us did not break; it did not even fray. The ordeal was Collyer's rather than mine. The tension must often

have been severe. But always it yielded to the patience, gentleness, and good will which made him the man he was. There
was much of sanctity in him. On my side there was an adoration which did not linger in my heart till death to manifest
itself too late. In me and in the congregation, as long as he
lived, there was perfect accord, a sweet content of spirit. When
he died, there was the passing of a bodily presence which had
done well for nearly ninety years, and of a spiritual power which
was strangely with us still.

Dr. Collyer was a man of striking appearance. In the full
vigor of his manhood he stood tall, with shoulders and arms
made of heroic proportions by the long years of labor at the
anvil. His literary style both in speaking and writing was unique
for its utter Anglo-Saxon purity. To hear or read him was to be
carried back to the pages of *Pilgrim's Progress* or the King
James Bible. His understanding of the human heart was as a
shining light through all his speech, and his simple love of men
was a benediction. As age developed, he became one of the
handsomest and most venerable of old men. His great frame,
his snow-white hair, his benignant features, his clear voice,
tended to make him a person never to be forgotten.

At last, in February, 1907, he was relieved when [I] became
minister of the church. The following summer he made his
eighth visit to Europe, and was crowned with the degree of
Doctor of Literature by Victoria University, Leeds. In 1911 he
was given the degree of Doctor of Divinity by the Meadville
Theological School. In the eighty-ninth year of his age he died,
after a month's illness, on November 30, 1912.

He gave into my hands a torch which was undimmed—he
placed in my keeping a sacred fire that still glowed with light
and warmth. If Dr. [Orville G.] Dewey is fittingly characterized
as the father of the Church of the Messiah, I believe that Dr.
Collyer must be described as its savior, or, perhaps, still better,

its second father! This church, as it lives and moves and has its being today, is Robert Collyer's church. It is his, for he made it. We are the sheep of his pasture, and the people of his hand!

> I Speak for Myself, 1958; essay, "Robert Collyer," 1917, in symposium, Heralds of a Liberal Faith, 1952; sermon, "In Memoriam: Robert Collyer," The Messiah Pulpit, 1915

EUGENE V. DEBS
(1855–1926)

On November 28, 1919, Eugene V. Debs wrote to John Haynes Holmes from the Federal Penitentiary in Atlanta, Georgia, to thank him for his "very kind and beautiful letter" and said that he had been "particularly impressed by your courageous and altogether noble attitude at the beginning of this war, an attitude of moral loftiness and genuine patriotism which you have maintained with unfaltering rectitude and devotion ever since."

Several months later Debs wrote a note to his wife on the back of an envelope which had come to him in the penitentiary in mid-April from Holmes:

> Please acknowledge for me this perfectly beautiful testimonial from this perfectly great and splendid soul. I catch the full fine spirit of him across the wide spaces and feel myself thrilled and exalted. Were I but half worthy of such noble praise! Please say that if I lived near his church, I'd be a church member for the first time in my life. I have his [Community Church of New York] "Calendar" on the wall

*in my prison chamber with his portrait and fine sayings, and
I commune with him every day.*

It is a fitting commentary on the spiritual condition of
America today, a startling revelation of the character of the age
in which we live, a true index of the sincerity of the religion
which we profess, that the purest, bravest, noblest man among
all the one hundred and ten millions of our people, is sleeping
this night [April 13, 1921] behind the bars of a prison cell. Of
all who breathe the atmosphere of earth, there is no gentler
soul than Eugene V. Debs, none who loves his fellow-men more
truly, none who has served the cause of truth more valiantly,
none who embodies within himself more clearly the ideal of
"peace on earth, good will to men." And yet, for this man in
America today we have no place but a penitentiary at Atlanta,
as for such a man in Palestine two thousand years ago there was
no place but a cross on Calvary!

Of what is Debs guilty that he should be so punished? Guilty
of no offense even under the Espionage Act, for he communi-
cated no secrets to the enemy, interfered with no processes of
war, encouraged no resistance to government! His crime was a
constructive crime, tortured into indictment, persecution and
conviction by officers of law acting under the influence of the
mad hysteria of wartime. His real offense was in the moral, not
the legal field. He was guilty of seeing what all honest men now
see when it is too late, that the Great War [1914–18] was a
selfish, lustful struggle between brigand nations, in which there
was involved no vestige of an ideal for which it was worth while
shedding the blood of a single soldier! Guilty of stating publicly,
when it was worth stating and therefore perilous, what all men
are now confessing privately when it is safe, that war is futile,
bringing as little good to those who win as to those who lose!
Guilty of loving men with a heart so overflowing with pity and

devotion, that he could not see them schooled in hate, trained to murder, sent like cattle to the slaughter-pen, without voicing a protest acceptable to God if not to government! The guilt of Debs is the guilt of every man who has trod the path of martyr-dom—the guilt of Socrates, of Jeremiah, of Jesus, of Savonarola and John Huss, of Lloyd Garrison, Leo Tolstoi and Karl Liebknecht. It is the guilt of words—words which seem to do nothing but as a matter of fact do everything, words which face men with the truth when they least want to see it, which tell men of their sins when they would most forget them, which remind men of their God when they are farthest from him. The true words of a true man are more terrible than swords and bayonets. Men fear them as they fear the lightning-blast of the Day of Judgment.

. . . His words were a judgment on men who were eaten up with hate and crazed with fear. They were a mirror in which the people were made to see the nakedness of their shame. Debs told the truth, which is the one unpardonable sin. Even in ordinary times, and in the case of an ordinary man, to tell the truth means loss of friends, of reputation, of money, of social standing. In times of terror, and in the case of a man who has on his tongue the fire of a prophet and in his heart the holiness of a saint, to tell the truth means death. For the American people, during the war, to live with Debs was as impossible as to live with Christ. They therefore got rid of both!

Address at Amnesty Mass Meeting, Washington, published in *Unity*, April 21, 1921

. . . I loved 'Gene Debs to the very bottom of my soul; I honored him above all other men now alive in America; I should count myself as faithless to my task, and faithless to the professed ideals of this church, did I not proclaim at this time my sorrow for his passing [October 20, 1926]. I feel, as it were, like some priest, bringing to you some precious treasures from his altar. . . .

And now he's dead—dear old 'Gene! I cannot be sad for him, for I know the labor of his days, and how richly he has earned his rest. I can only be sad for a nation, for a world, that dictated contempt, denunciation, ridicule, imprisonment, and untimely death for such a man. Do you remember the closing scene of Bernard Shaw's *Saint Joan*, when the Maid, risen from her martyrdom, proposes to come back to earth? Rebuked by her worshipers, who shrink one by one away, the sainted girl, deserted once again, lifts to heaven that pitiful prayer, upon which the curtain falls, "O God, who hast made this beautiful earth, when will it be ready to receive thy saints? How long, O Lord, how long?"

I fear it will be long, if not forever. But fortunately this earth, however "beautiful," is not all. There are immortalities beyond. . . .

Sermon, "Debs—Lover of Men,"
The Community Pulpit, 1926

CLARENCE DARROW
(1857–1938)

In the fall of 1926 Clarence Darrow was invited by a number of associates and followers of John Haynes Holmes to join them in paying tribute to their friend's imminent twentieth anniversary as minister of the Community Church of New York; and in response he wrote: "Few men in any generation have been so devoted to the cause of freedom and so true to his ideals as Dr. Holmes has been. In a world of intolerance, brutality and bigotry, he has dared to proclaim the truth as he sees it and understands it. He is one of the few men down through the ages to whom humanity owes a deep feeling of appreciation and gratitude. The poor and weak and oppressed will have an able defender so long as he lives.

Three years later, when Holmes asked Darrow to "share some wisdom" with the audience of the church's Sunday Evening Forum, the Chicago attorney accepted the invitation with a reservation: ". . . I am afraid I am not growing to be a sage; just growing old. Still, old age isn't so bad."

In 1931, acknowledging Holmes's congratulations on the occasion of his seventy-fourth birthday, he penned a note to say: "I have not forgotten your eloquent words when you came out from New York to help celebrate my 70th birthday. Your friendship is one of the most satisfying of all my relations with my fellows. Somehow, it never makes much difference to me whether we agree or not. We feel alike on the big things of life and that is enough."

It is difficult to think of any other American of this generation who would be so widely mourned and by such various groups of persons as the great Chicago lawyer. Rich and poor stood side by side at his bier; Christian and atheist recognized and reverenced in him qualities of manhood which strangely made them one; conservative and radical ceased their contentions in his presence and before his memory; Negro, Jew, the workingman, and all the struggling and oppressed of earth found in him a brother. Darrow was sharp of tongue, ironic in thought and speech, a pessimist and unbeliever, but he had a heart as tender as a child's which could exclude no man from its sympathy. He would have denied the truth of the famous hymn—

There's a wideness in God's mercy,
   Like the wideness of the sea, . . .

for the world to him seemed cruel, and God, if there is a God, a callous and indifferent ruler. But in his own soul he revealed the divine compassion. In his own life he demonstrated the reality of the religion which he denied. Hence did all men rally to him and revere him.

In his thought processes, Clarence Darrow was a curious survivor of an age which passed without his realizing it. For some reason he never kept up at all with the progress of human knowledge. In his great old age he stood exactly at the point where he had stood in his early rebellious manhood. When he discussed great problems of being and destiny, and vast issues of individual and social life, it was as though the clock had been turned back and we were returned to the days of the mid-Victorians.

Thus, in his religious thought, he moved in the realm of early-nineteenth-century agnosticism. Even this agnosticism was not clear, since it was mingled with a crude materialism which came from one knew not where. Darrow had learned in his young manhood, at second and third hand, that there was a Biblical criticism which was discrediting the infallibility of the Scriptures, a science which had overthrown the theological dogmas of creation, a philosophy which was casting doubts upon traditional ideas of God, the soul, and immortality. These rumors, which he seldom confirmed beyond their popularization in many forms, matched perfectly his own instinctive revolt against a traditional religion which his sound sensibility taught him was at once irrational and immoral, and out of them he built a structure of doubt or denial, which lasted him without change to the end of his days.

One saw this dramatized in unforgettable fashion in the famous "monkey trial" in Dayton, Tennessee, when Bryan and Darrow engaged in their theological passage at arms. Here were two men who were hopelessly behind the times—Bryan with a belief as antiquated as the lore of the medieval Schoolmen,

Darrow with an unbelief as crude as the jimcracks of the old-time village atheist. Neither one knew that the world both of belief and unbelief had moved to a point so remote from their vision as not to be seen at all. And so, like two warriors battling with bows and arrows in the day of machine-guns, these two doughty champions fought their duel, Darrow coming off triumphant through a native shrewdness of intellect for which Bryan's simple faith could be no match.

The same thing was true of Clarence Darrow's political philosophy. He was reared as a young man and trained as a young lawyer in the heyday of the *laissez-faire* school of thought. This thought had its rootage in England in the early capitalistic industrialism which flourished in Manchester and other great mill towns. In this country it found fresh and fertile soil in the new agricultural frontier. Here flourished in fullest and fairest flower the characteristic individualism of the nineteenth century. On the positive side, this individualism found expression in a personal independence, self-reliance and initiative which constitute America's chief contribution to the life of modern times. On the negative side, it took the form of a distrust and even hatred of government which is the real philosophical foundation of the principle of anarchy. As Darrow was an unbeliever in the field of religion of the distinctive mid-nineteenth-century type, so he was a philosophical anarchist in the field of politics of the same type. And in the one case as in the other, it was his instinct, nurtured by more or less indirect environmental influences, which led him early to fixed conclusions which never altered.

Born and reared in a small Mid-Western town, early acquainted with political corruption, vulgarity, and oppression, Darrow revolted from the State as he had revolted from the Church, and asked only to be left alone. But the State did not, because it could not, leave him or other men alone. With the growing complexity of human relationships, government became more and more a factor in men's lives. Inevitably, with the disappearance of the frontier, individualism began steadily to move toward socialization. Our problems, whether we would have them so or not, became social problems and our methods social methods. But Darrow would not have it so, and to the end of his days fought the fate-like tendencies of the time. Many of his most passionate interests were rooted not merely in his moral idealism and his human pity, but also and quite as much in his distrust of government. He hated and denounced Prohibition because it was an invasion by the State of the liberties of the individual. He fought capital punishment because it was the State laying its bloody hand upon some poor forlorn individual whom it had earlier betrayed by neglect or oppression. He served as a lawyer always on the side of the defendant because, among other things, this was one way of resisting the encroachments of government upon the life of the single man. This was pure individualism of the extreme *laissez-faire* variety. It has its attraction in this day of dictators and totalitarian states. But it represents a type of thought and way of life which vanished long before Clarence Darrow finished his career.

Clarence Darrow was thus in certain ways a curious, if very precious, museum piece. He was an heroic, if frustrated, survivor of an age which he could not recognize and would not accept. It was this fact, coupled with certain qualities of inner temperament, which made him a pessimist—the most lovable pessimist who ever lived, but still a pessimist. This world was to him a mad and cruel world. There was no sense nor sanity in it. Especially was there no pity. But men needed pity, just because they were living helplessly in such a world. And this pity Darrow himself proposed to supply, since the cosmos itself was pitiless. Thereupon appeared in action such a piteous heart as mankind has seldom known.

There were no limits to Darrow's compassion. It reached

everywhere—touched every life. Nobody was too mean to receive his attention—nobody too wicked to be worthy of his understanding. The underdog was his especial friend, the downtrodden and oppressed his brethren, the outcast and wretched and despised his loved ones. Not since Saint Francis walked this earth has the world seen such mercy clad in human flesh. Not since Jesus himself has there been such an exemplar of the gospel of "unto this last." If religion is love, as it surely is, then Clarence Darrow was one of the most religious men who ever lived, and his pessimism a purer wellspring of the spirit than all the founts of faith.

There were qualities in Darrow's heart which were deeper far than the accidents of thought and incidents of experience which conspired to clothe his life in so deceptive a garb. There were times when the sheer beauty of his life so denied the grim negations of his speech that it seemed as though the great man were playing a part in some sardonic spirit of raillery or jest. But in word as in deed, Darrow was magnificently sincere, and his life all of a piece. Central to everything else within him was a tenderness as of a woman. It was this tenderness which moved him to revolt against a hell-fire theology which taught a vindictive God who wreaked punishment upon helpless humankind, and against a corrupt politics which used the State as a weapon to humiliate, oppress and exploit its baffled citizens. To thwart and defeat this conspiracy of the strong against the weak, of the favored against the underprivileged, of the respectable and pious against the disreputable and sinful—a conspiracy begun in this world and continued into the next—this became the high mission of his days.

And what a fighter he was! One sees him in the court of law or on the platform of public debate, his great head thrust forward upon his hunched shoulders, his hands thrust deep into the pockets of his baggy trousers, his quiet eyes gazing straight and true from out the shadow of his beetling brows, his calm, still voice shooting its shafts of bitter irony, devastating wit, or passionate appeal, his huge frame quivering with indignation against some potent iniquity, his stern, deeply lined and infinitely beautiful face glowing with compassion for some lost cause or lost soul. Never was there a more dangerous antagonist—a moment's carelessness, and his swift sword was dealing a death-thrust under the guard! Never was a dearer, truer, more loving friend—in his hand-clasp was an affection which absorbed all alien interests and differing opinions! His tenderness was instant to every need; because so sensitive, it could not endure with complacency the woes of humankind. And so the great heart cried out in sheer horror and denunciation, and in the very darkness of its own pain revealed the saving light of love.

Darrow's thought and life were compounded throughout of irony. The final irony was left for the last, when he who had ridiculed and rejected all religion became suddenly the pattern of the religious life. For religion tells of a Day of Judgment when men shall be brought before the throne of Christ to render account of their deeds upon the earth. Darrow must stand there among the rest, and hear the words, "I was hungry, and ye gave me meat; I was thirsty, and ye gave me drink; I was a stranger, and ye took me in; naked, and ye clothed me; I was sick, and ye visited me; I was in prison, and ye came unto me." No one of all that company will be more surprised at these words than Clarence Darrow. He will give those mighty shoulders an extra hunch, edge that quiet voice with its most quizzical drawl, and ask, "Lord, when saw I thee anhungered, and fed thee; or thirsty, and gave thee drink; when saw I thee a stranger, and took thee in; or naked, and clothed thee; or when saw I thee sick, or in prison, and came unto thee?" And will the great head drop in sweet humility, or lift in glad surprise, when there comes the immortal answer, "Inasmuch as ye did it unto the least of these, my brethren, ye did it unto me"?   Editorial in *Unity*, May 16, 1938

MOHANDAS KARAMCHAND GANDHI
(1869–1948)

One of the great regrets of Holmes's life in the later years was his inability to locate the correspondence between Mahatma Gandhi and himself, for the twenty-five years' exchange of letters vanished during the many transitions of the Community Church offices from one location to another in the 1920s, '30s, and early '40s. Those precious letters may be extant somewhere, but to the present time they have not appeared. Apart from a few tantalizingly brief letters, Holmes had to content himself with his vivid memories of the memorable meetings he had with Gandhi in 1931 and 1947, the comforting awareness that they had frequently been in touch with each other through the crisis-laden years, and the assurance given him by greetings brought from the Mahatma by such a friend of both men as Jane Addams of Chicago's Hull-House. In 1923 Miss Addams had written from Delhi that she had just seen Gandhi and spent some time at his spinning school, "a beautiful spot in the midst of huge experimental cotton fields, . . . like the beginnings of a religious order, as the Franciscans must have been before St. Francis' death."

In the autograph collection Holmes kept as a hobby there is a brief letter from Gandhi saying, "There is no certainty about my going to London as yet [to the Round Table Conference]. There are difficulties which may prove insuperable. I feel that I must not leave India unless some glaring breaches of the Settlement are repaired. I am straining every nerve to avoid a conflict, but the result is in God's hands. But if I do succeed in going to London we must meet." [Early summer, 1931.]

Another note in Gandhi's handwriting came in the spring of 1944, when he responded to Holmes's word of sympathy on the death of his wife: "I was much touched by your letter of

10th May last. Dissolution of my wife's body has enriched my life, for I remember only her great merits. Her limitations were reduced to ashes with her body." Noting that "we are all passing through anxious times," Gandhi concluded the letter with the words: "Sympathy of friends like you sustains me in my struggle against evil."

In the summer of 1947 Gandhi wrote Holmes: "We are all looking forward to your arrival [in India]." The last communication from the Mahatma arrived in mid-January 1948 and recalled with pleasure Holmes's visits in his quarters in New Delhi during the previous autumn. It contained a reprint of an editorial Gandhi had written in acknowledgment of a tribute Holmes had paid to the Gandhian devotion to Ahimsa, the principle of nonviolence, and concluded with a question to his readers: "Have I attained the requisite qualifications for exhibiting the virtues of Ahimsa as Dr. Holmes believes?"

Twenty-seven days after Gandhi wrote that letter and asked the question, he lay dead at the hands of an assassin.

I Discover Gandhi

On a certain day in 1918, I went to the New York Public Library to read an article in the current issue of the *Hibbert Journal* . . . which had been commended to my attention. The article in question was by Sir Gilbert Murray, on the subject, "The Soul as It Is, and How to Deal with It." It was in substance a study of conscientious objection in wartime, especially as dramatized in the person of the English Quaker Stephen Hobhouse. But right along with Hobhouse appeared a reference to an Indian by the name of Mohandas Karamchand Gandhi, of whom I had never until this moment heard. Professor Murray did not seem to know any too much about the man either. "I am told," he wrote, "that Gandhi's influence in India is now enormous, almost equal to that of his friend, the late Mr. Gokhale." But in the space of two pages he told the epic saga of Gandhi's nonviolent campaign in South Africa through two decades (1893–1914) against the white man's government and on behalf of his downtrodden fellow countrymen, the dark-skinned coolies, and this was enough to identify the Indian leader as a heroic, and incidentally successful, practitioner of spiritual force as contrasted with physical or armed force. Murray saw the likeness of Gandhi to Stephen Hobhouse in his reliance upon the soul as the supreme instance of the adaptation of means to ends. Such men are dangerous to any existing *status quo,* and to all injustice and tyranny. Moved by Gandhi's exploits in South Africa, Murray wrote in comment upon the significance of this Indian:

> Persons in power should be very careful how they deal with a man who cares nothing for sensual pleasure, nothing for riches, nothing for comfort or praise or promotion, but is simply determined to do what he believes to be right. He is a dangerous and uncomfortable enemy—because his body, which you can always conquer, gives you so little purchase upon his soul.

It was amid this growing confusion and dismay [of the First World War] that there emerged from my mind that *Hibbert Journal* article, especially in its Gandhi section, which I had read at just the critical moment when America had entered and was fighting the Great War. Its recollection sprang out of my dire personal need. It had lain dormant, like a scattered seed, all these months gone by. It was now quickened again by my receiving, at just this moment, and more or less fortuitously, a little paper-covered pamphlet, somewhat the worse for wear, containing some addresses and letters by M. K. Gandhi, of India. Instantly I seemed to be alive—my vision clear, my mind at peace, my heart reassured. Here was the perfect answer to all my problems. I ran back to the library, and read again Professor Murray's article. Instantly something clicked within me, like the turning of a lock. Before I knew it, the supreme moment of my life had come. . . .

There was little in what Professor Murray had written to satisfy my curiosity. But this little was quite enough to prod me wide awake, and to shake me, like a midnight earthquake, to the very foundations of my being. I lived the experience of John Keats when he first read Chapman's Homer and wrote his immortal confession,

> Then felt I like some watcher of the skies
> When a new planet swims into his ken.

I left the library that afternoon in a daze of wonder and excitement. I must learn about this man whom I had so unexpectedly discovered. I must get information to dispel my ignorance. But my quest proved to be difficult. People in general and scholars in particular seemed to know as little about this Indian in South Africa as I did. For Gandhi had not broken into the magic circle of the public press. He had not yet attracted the attention of journalists who hold the key to the closed door of contemporary knowledge. There was material, of course, published in South Africa, but this was mostly inaccessible in America. Not until I went to England in 1922, did I lay hold on some of this material, and have the great good fortune to meet Mr. Henry S. L. Polak, early associate of Gandhi, who was the first to write of him. My search, however, proved to be mostly an experience of frustration. But all the while, in my early bafflement and occasional despair, I felt within me the ever-deepening conviction that I was on the right track. This Gandhi was a great and wonderful man. Where was there anybody to match him in our troubled and wicked world? Did he not hold in his heart the secret of man's deliverance from the evils, mostly of man's own choosing, which were now besetting him and threatening to destroy him? Must he not be proclaimed at once as a world leader, the compeer of the greatest men of our own or any other time?

The more I thought of it, the more this conviction grew upon me. It was under its impress—an intuition of the soul rather than any persuasion of the mind—that I climbed tremulously into my pulpit on Sunday morning, April 10, 1921, to preach to my people on the subject "Who Is the Greatest Man in the World?" and to answer my own question, M. K. Gandhi, of India.

My Gandhi, 1953

Who Is the Greatest Man in the World Today?

"I believe absolutely," says Gandhi, "that India has a mission for the world." His idealism, therefore, transcends the boundaries of race and country, and seeks to make itself one with the highest hope of humanity. "My religion" he cries, "has no geographical limits. If I have a living faith in it, it will transcend my love for India herself."

Such is Mahatma Gandhi! In this great spirit, he lives among the people. As he moves from city to city, crowds of thirty and even fifty thousand people assemble to hear his words. As he pauses for the night in a village, or in the open countryside, great throngs come to him as to a holy shrine. He would seem to be what the Indians regard him—the perfect and universal man. In his personal character, he is simple and undefiled. In his political endeavors, he is as stern a realist as Lenin, working steadfastly toward a far goal of liberation which must be won. At the same time, however, is he an idealist, like Romain Rolland, living ever in the pure radiance of the spirit. When I think of Rolland, as I have said, I think of Tolstoi. When I think of Lenin, I think of Napoleon. But when I think of Gandhi, I think of Jesus Christ. He lives his life; he speaks his word; he suffers, strives and will some day nobly die, for his kingdom upon earth.

Do you recall how it told of Jesus, that one day, as he was journeying, he heard his disciples quarrelling? And he said, "What were ye reasoning on the way?" And they said they had disputed, who was the greatest. And Jesus said, "If any man would be first among you, let him be the servant of all."

Sermon, *The Community Pulpit*,

1921

The World Significance of Mahatma Gandhi

Gandhi is a man who has mastered the secrets of spiritual living. His soul has been lifted, by virtue of incomparable discipline, to the measure of the stature of those realities which are of God. In humility, in sacrifice, in ardent love for men, he is one of those perfect characters which come along once in a thousand, or perhaps only in two thousand, years. And today he lies in prison. Such men are the judges of our world. A society which cannot suffer a Jesus or a Gandhi to be at large is a society which is not fit to live, and by this token is already doomed to die.

At the heart of this Western civilization of ours, Gandhi believes, is death and not life. We have created a vast machine which proves to be a Frankenstein which is devouring us. This monster has bound us to the wheel of labor, deceived us with the lure of wealth, degraded us to the base uses of materialism, leveled to the ground our standards of moral and spiritual idealism. Even in a physical sense it is a failure, for in the end it brings only such calamity as the Great War. It is this system of economic ruin which Gandhi sees coming into Asia, after having conquered and ravaged our Western world. He sees it victorious in Japan, he sees it invading China, he sees it planted at the heart of India—*and he declares war against it!* He fights the opium trade, he battles against the liquor traffic, he substitutes the domestic spindle for the factory loom, he denounces the railroad, the automobile and the machine in general. What Gandhi is attempting to do is save India from the blight of Western materialism by restoring her own native civilization and culture before it is too late. He is trying to preserve his land from the curse of commercialism, the horror of machine exploitation and production, the slavery of wage labor, the whole black system of capitalistic life. And he would do this not for its own sake, but for the sake of India's soul. He would save the spirit of his people—their simplicity, their art, their religion, their mystic comradeship with one another and with God.

It is in this work of spiritual redemption that he takes on a universal significance, for the West as well as for the East. For in saving India, Gandhi is saving the world. In staying the ravages of capitalism in his own land, he is starting a movement which, by process of reaction, will flow back into our world and restore to us those things of the spirit which we have lost. Our Western civilization is in exactly the situation of Rome in the days of the great Caesar. It has mastered the world by the power of its arms, and is exploiting its resources and peoples to its own advantage. As its outward glory increases, however, its inward disintegration proceeds. At the critical moment in Roman history, there appeared Jesus and the Christians, who brought to the perishing world a new source of life which preserved its vitality for a period of two thousand years. At the critical moment in our not dissimilar age, there appears Gandhi! Does he not also bring with him a new life of the spirit, and may he not therefore be truly hailed as the savior of the world?

It is thus that I would speak of the universal significance of Mahatma Gandhi and his work in India. The parallel with Jesus constantly presents itself. The Nazarene was a divine

personality; he taught the law of love, and laid down a program
of non-resistance for its fulfillment; he sought to establish the
Kingdom of Heaven on earth by dethroning Mammon in favor
of God. So also with Gandhi! This Indian is a saint in his
personal life; he teaches the law of love, and non-resistance as
its practice; and he seeks the establishment of a new social
order which shall be a kingdom of the spirit. If I believed in
"the second coming," as I do not, I should dare to assert that
Gandhi was Jesus come back to earth. But if "the second
coming" has no historical validity, it has at least poetical significance; and in this sense can we not speak of Gandhi as
indeed the Christ?

Sermon, *The Community Pulpit,*
1922

I Meet Gandhi

I have met Gandhi—have clasped his hand, have looked into
his eyes, have listened to his voice. I have sat in a great public
audience, and heard him speak; I have sat alone at his feet and
talked with him about many things. . . . I saw Gandhi at the
climactic hour of his career, and against the background of
events momentous in the history not only of our own but of
all time. I can tell you, therefore, not only of my impressions
of the man, but also of my estimate of his significance today
for India, the Empire, and the world. I have met, in other
words, not merely an individual, but a cause, a movement, a
revolution. How do I feel about this phenomenon—this Word
become flesh which dwells among us "full of grace and truth"—
this incarnation of the Spirit in which is life, and this life "the
light of men"?

I was in Berlin when I heard that Gandhi was coming to
London. Earlier in the summer I had received from him a letter

in which he had spoken of his journey, and of his expectation of seeing me on his arrival. But his plans had been thrown into confusion, and he had announced that he would not attend the Round Table Conference. Then came the agreement with the Viceroy, and the sudden determination to make the trip. The moment I heard that Gandhi was coming, that he had actually taken ship and was on the sea, I abandoned all my other arrangements and rushed to London, resolved to camp upon the Mahatma's threshold until the door might open and let me through. I had not dared to hope that I could greet him when first he landed upon English soil. But by a dramatic and amusing combination of circumstances, which is a story in itself, I found myself on the morning of Saturday, September 12th, standing on the pier at Folkstone, awaiting the arrival of the Channel steamer.

It was typical English weather—cold and foggy, with occasional heavy showers. The wind was sweeping the waves with whitecaps, and chilling the bones of the watchers on the pier. I was talking with an officer, one of the members of the police force appointed to be the bodyguard of the Mahatma.

"Do you see that point of land over there," he said to me, pointing to the white cliffs of Dover to the north. "That's where Caesar landed when he brought his legions to conquer England."

To conquer England! I thought of that great soldier of ancient Rome and of his victories upon these shores. His Twentieth Legion had remained here three hundred years! Then I thought of another conqueror—William of Normandy— who had crossed this Channel a thousand years after the immortal Julius, and beaten the Saxons and annexed their realm. This invader had landed at Peveny, not so many miles here to the south. And now another thousand years had passed, and still another conqueror was crossing these stormy seas. Not a soldier, but mightier than any soldier. Not an invader, with a sword of steel, but an apostle with the sword of the spirit. Not an enemy to lay waste the land, but a friend to surprise and devastate the hearts of Englishmen. If ever Britain was in peril, it was in peril now, when for the third time in two thousand years, there was coming an alien to dictate terms of peace.

I wiped the rain from my glasses, and gazed out through the mist to the open sea. There was the steamer, a little craft in white, emerging from the horizon like a sheeted ghost. As she made fast at the pier, only one man, the official representative of the British government, was allowed on board. All the rest of us—friends of Gandhi, delegates from India, the Dean of Canterbury, newspaper reporters and photographers—were left standing in the rain, with a great crowd of sight-seers behind the barriers. But the delay was brief. In a few moments we were aboard the ship, and I was standing at the door of Gandhi's cabin awaiting my turn to be received. It was here I had my first glimpse of the Mahatma. He was sitting cross-legged upon his berth, in earnest conversation with Reginald Reynolds, a young English Quaker who had been a resident at the Ashram in India, and had become famous as the bearer of Gandhi's letter to the Viceroy on the eve of the march to Dandi. Gandhi's legs were bare, his body wrapped to the neck in the ample folds of a Khaddar shawl. His head and shoulders were bent forward in a listening attitude. A naked arm, long and lean and wiry, reached out of the shawl and took a paper from Reynolds' hand. There was a quick interchange of words, a flitting smile, and the conference was over.

It was now my turn. I stepped into the little cabin. Instantly Gandhi jumped to his feet, and, with the lithe, quick step of a schoolboy, came forward to greet me. I felt his hands take mine in a grasp as firm as that of an athlete. I saw his eyes shining with a light so bright that not even the thick glass of his rude spectacles could obscure their radiance. I heard his voice addressing me in tones as rich and full as they were gentle. We had a few precious moments together. I was confused and excited, and today have little memory of what was said. But at this first meeting it was not words but feelings that were important. I was in the presence of the man whose spirit had reached me, years before, across the continents and seas of half the world, and now this presence was stamping its indelible impression upon my mind.

What was this first impression of Gandhi, as distinguished from the others which came later? I do not find it difficult to answer this question. It was an impression of the beauty of the man. Where do people get the idea that Gandhi is ugly? Why have they described him as a "dwarf," and a "little monkey of a man"? It is true that his limbs and body are emaciated—his ascetic life produces no surplus flesh! But his frame is large, and his stature erect and of medium height; I have seen many Indians who are much more insignificant in appearance than Mahatma Gandhi. It is true also that his individual features are not lovely. He has a shaven head, protruding ears, thick lips, and a mouth that is minus many of its teeth. But his dark complexion is richly beautiful against the white background of his shawl, his eyes shine like candles in the night, and over all is the radiance of a smile like sunshine on a morning land- scape. What impresses you is not the physical appearance but the spiritual presence of this man. You think at once of his simplicity, his sincerity, his innocence. He approaches you with all the naturalness and spontaneity of a little child. There is not an atom of self-consciousness in Gandhi—in spite of all his greatness in the world, and all the adulation which has been heaped upon him, he has no pose, no pretentiousness, no pride. You realize at once that his peculiar aspects of appearance and his peculiar ways of life have nothing fraudulent about them, but are the honest and fearless expression of a transcendent personality. Therefore you do not think of how he looks, but only of what he is. You see truth, in other words, shining through the imperfect garment of the flesh. It is that which makes Gandhi beautiful. For truth is beauty! You remember how John Keats told us this in the closing lines of his great "Ode on a Grecian Urn," when he wrote

Beauty is truth, truth beauty,—that is all
Ye know on earth, and all ye need to know.

In a few moments we were off the boat, and started for London. Gandhi was in the official automobile of the government, guarded by police. I rode in a compartment of the train with Devidas Gandhi, the Mahatma's son, Mr. Pyarelal, one of his secretaries, and Miss Madeleine Slade, the English girl, now known as Mirabai, his servant and disciple.

We were soon in London, and went immediately through the mud and rain to the Friends Meeting House, where a great audience had gathered to meet and welcome Gandhi. As I saw him enter this auditorium, I was impressed again by the beauty of his personality, and now, also, by its power. With what dignity he walked upon this platform; with what serenity he surveyed this English scene; with what command he took possession of these men and women! To an intruder who knew nothing of Gandhi, nor of the momentous character of the occasion, there might have been something ridiculous in the picture. Here was this Indian striding into the room with his feet bare, his legs naked to the thighs, his middle bound by the loin-cloth, his body wrapped and rewrapped in the ample folds of his Khaddar shawl. But as he took his seat, and sat there calm and motionless as Buddha, the ridiculous, if it ever was present, was straightway diffused and dissolved into the sublime. I shall never forget the sense of awe that settled like an atmosphere upon that room. For the first time I understood the secret of Gandhi's influence over the millions of his fellow-countrymen. Had a king been present, we could not have felt more reverence in his presence. Suddenly I found myself remembering the testimony of Mr. Bernay, a sensitive English journalist, who said, "The moment you see Gandhi, you catch the atmosphere of royalty." And I remembered also that, a few weeks before, I had been in the presence of royalty. I had seen and talked with the man who, for more than thirty years, had been the most brilliant monarch of his day. This man was nobly dressed, attended by his court, himself a fascinating, gracious, and splendid figure. But not all the majesty of this king could match the royal air of Gandhi.

But Gandhi not only looked like a king, he spoke like a king. His words that afternoon were gently uttered, in a voice quiet, almost monotonous. But as they reached our ears, they were the words of a royal proclamation. He made three points clear. First, his credentials! He came to England, he said, not as an individual, but as the representative of his people. "I represent, without any fear of contradiction, the dumb, semi-starved millions of India." Secondly, his mandate! He came not to dicker or to bargain with Britain, but to present the terms of the All-India Congress. "As an agent holding a power of attorney from the Congress," he said, "I shall have my limitations. I have to conduct myself within the four corners of the mandate I have received from the Congress . . . If I am to be loyal to the trust which has been put in me, I must not go outside that mandate." Lastly, his goal! What did the mandate exact? "Freedom," said Gandhi. "The Congress wants freedom unadulterated for these dumb and semi-starved millions." No compromise here, no equivocation! "He spake as one having authority"—and with the voice of prophecy.

This was on a Saturday afternoon. On the succeeding five days that I was privileged to remain in London, I saw the Mahatma four separate times. The first time was on the following morning, Sunday, when I went bright and early to Kingsley Hall, the settlement house in the east end of London where

Gandhi had characteristically taken up his abode. He was on an open terrace just outside his room, which was a kind of cell some five feet wide, seven or eight feet long, with stone floor and bare walls, and furnished only with a table, a chair, and a thin pallet on the floor where Gandhi slept. Mirabai was washing the one window of the little room. The Mahatma was sitting on a chair, bathed in the warm sunshine of a perfect day. He was talking with one of the great leaders of Indian affairs. Within a few moments this conference was finished, and I came and sat down in a chair beside the Mahatma. We talked of the Round Table Conference—was it going to succeed? No, Gandhi saw no reason for believing that it would succeed. His mind told him it must fail. "But God has told me to come to England," he said, very simply, "and he must have his own reasons. So I have put my mind aside, and shall trust and hope until the end." I referred to the slanderous attacks upon him in certain of the London newspapers, and expressed the hope that they did not trouble him. "No," he said, "they do not trouble me, but they pain me terribly. Think of how fully and freely I have talked to the reporters. I have told them everything. And yet they print these slanders and vicious lies. It hurts me to think that such things can be done. But," he continued, with a smile, "I do not let them worry me. They do no harm. Nothing can injure truth." I then referred to the next day, Monday, which was his day of silence, and asked if he would attend the Conference. "Oh, yes," he said, with his delightful smile now become almost a laugh, "I shan't say a word, but think what a chance I shall have to listen." We talked of a few other matters, and then I arose with an apology that I had taken his time, for others were waiting to see him, as indeed they always are. I shall never forget the loveliness of his smile, as he took my hand, and said, "Come whenever you can. You may have to wait, but I want to see you as long as you are in London."

I next saw Gandhi on Sunday night at a religious service in which his friends and some men and women from the neighborhood participated. The Mahatma sat on the platform, not in a chair but on the floor, wrapped in a shawl, with a rug thrown about his bare legs. He spoke to us, from his sitting posture, on prayer, his experience of prayer. He stated that he believed in God, and therefore of course prayed. He told us what prayer had done for him. "Without prayer," he said, "I could do nothing." As he went on in his quiet way, telling us of his experience with this most intimate discipline of the spiritual life, his voice became very soft and low. I doubt if many persons in the room, back of the front rows where I was sitting, could hear what he was saying. The Mahatma seemed more and more to sink into himself. His address became a process of self-communion, or communion, right there before our eyes, with One greater than ourselves. But words were not necessary at such an hour! Gandhi's presence was diffusing an atmosphere in the little room which gripped us in its spell. It was a moment of mystic uplift never to be forgotten.

I did not see Gandhi again until Wednesday night, when I sat with him in his room during his supper hour. He was sitting on his bed, on the floor. I squatted down beside him, that I might be as near to him as possible. He held in his left hand a cup of goat's milk. On his lap was a tin plate, such as I have seen convicts use in a prison, and in this was the handful of dates which made the substance of his meal. Gandhi's secretary, Mr. Pyarelal, was with us but did not join in the conversation. We talked of many things—of the Round Table Conference, of [New York's] Mayor [James J.] Walker's request for an interview, of Palestine and Zionism and their relation to the situation in India, and of the Mahatma's projected visit to America. At the close, I bade him good-bye, for I was leaving on Friday, and did not expect to see him again. Immediately he laid aside his cup and plate, and took my hand in both of his. "We shall meet again," he said, "in America, or perhaps in India. But if we never meet, we shall still be together."

The next night, Thursday, Devidas Gandhi sought me out and told me, to my surprise, that his father wanted to see me. The Mahatma was at St. James's Palace, where the Round Table Conference held its sessions. I hastened with Devidas to the Palace, and found Gandhi in one of the committee rooms, eating his supper. He was sitting on a large lounge, or divan, and he invited me to sit down beside him. A message had come from America, and he wanted to discuss it with me. We talked for a half-hour or so, as members of Gandhi's party passed in and out of the room. Then, on word that the attendants were waiting to close the Palace, we all arose and started for the automobiles. Gandhi asked me if I would ride with him to Kingsley Hall. Of course I accepted his invitation, and sat by his side as we sped far eastward to the slum districts of the city. As we drew up to the house, we found the doorway blocked with a great crowd of children. The boys and girls of the neighborhood had become much excited over this strange man from India. In the morning they gathered in the street to see him drive away, and in the evening to see him come home again. This night it was late, but they were still there. And what a shout they raised as he emerged from the automobile! The Mahatma paused and turned toward the children with smiling face. They shouted again, and crowded about him to touch his hands and feel his shawl. I bade him a hasty good-bye, as he sought his room. And as I went down the narrow street, with the children's voices ringing in my ears, I thought of the story of one of Galilee, who said, "Suffer the little children to come unto me and forbid them not, for of such is the kingdom of heaven."

Sermon, *The Community Pulpit*,
1931

My Visit to India

On the very day of my arrival in New Delhi [in October, 1947] I was told that [Gandhi] had appointed an hour for me to see him. He was just around the corner from where I was staying, and it was easy to come knocking at his door. I was admitted at once, and found him sitting cross-legged on a snowy mattress on the floor, surrounded by pillows and cushions. He was troubled by a slight cough, but nevertheless wore nothing but his loincloth, and a light shawl draped over his bare shoulders and chest. He greeted me with that ineffable smile which is his loveliest feature, and we were soon chatting busily together. I thought him looking better than when I had seen him last, in London in 1931. He certainly was heavier, and his flesh was firm and all aglow with health. Only his voice was weak—at times I had some difficulty in hearing him. Perhaps this was because of the sadness which the impact of recent tragic events [riots following upon establishment of the independent nations of India and Pakistan] had impressed upon his soul. He spoke with anguish of the massacres, and especially of the refugees who were even then pouring into the city. But there was no bitterness, no despair, in what he said. He was shocked, but not for a moment overborne. His spirit was still triumphant, and single-handed was quieting the people. Never was Gandhi so great as at this hour; and never so simple and humble, and so truly brave, as when I saw him that afternoon in the midst of alarms. . . . This influence did not appear all at once. It was the fruitage of years of public discipline to non-violence. But when the crisis came, and it seemed as though all his work was to be undone, Gandhi faced the situation unperturbed. He commanded an end of strife, and was obeyed. He set an example of peace, and it was followed. He announced a fast in penance, and the nation bowed in shame. As

Jesus stilled the storm of the Sea of Galilee, so Gandhi stilled the storm of slaughter in India. Himself bowed down in sorrow, he arose to snatch victory from the jaws of defeat. I say advisedly that this was the supreme moment of the Mahatma's supreme career. . . . After a decent interval, I arose and left him. I saw him again that night at his regular prayer-meeting— and had a farewell talk with him when I left New Delhi. He was very tender and gracious with me that second afternoon. It was the one disappointment of my trip that engagements took me to other parts of the country, and I did not see him again.

But I felt him wherever I was. His presence was everywhere. His daily visitors are announced in the papers as in the court register of a king. His doings are reported with a precision of detail which puts to shame our reporting of our President. His evening prayer-meeting talks are taken down for transmission over the radio, and are published in every paper in the land. No public meeting but what his name is mentioned with reverence and gratitude. No private gathering but what he is referred to and praised. In the largest cities his word is a command, in the smallest villages an occasion of worship. Statesmen sit at his feet, and humble folk follow in his steps. Universally recognized as the liberator of his country, venerable in years and pure in spirit, he has outlived all criticism, all jealousy, all party feeling, and holds in his lifetime the prestige and power that posterity grants only to its sainted dead. I search in vain for any parallel to this universal recognition and exaltation of a single man. America's attitude toward Lincoln, Christianity's attitude toward Christ, this is India's attitude toward the Mahatma. And will some day be the world's!

Sermon, *The Community Pulpit,*
1947

After Gandhi's Death

When [Gandhi] fell beneath the assassin's bullet [on January 30, 1948], it seemed as though the very foundations of the universe cracked and swayed. I felt I had suffered irretrievable loss. For days the world seemed empty. Then a strange thing happened. I found that, in any thought and utterance, I was referring to Gandhi not in the past but in the present tense in my verbs—"Gandhi thinks so and so," "Gandhi says this or that"—just as though he had not died at all, but was living. As time went on, I discovered that this habit did not pass, but remained a persistent practice. The Mahatma was still my guide, counselor and friend. I took him my problems, just as I had before the fatal day, and always he replied. This was a spiritual experience as real as anything in the flesh. Gandhi was here—a living presence still.

The same is true of India. I am told that Gandhi is a greater influence over the Indian people today than ever he was in his own lifetime. His words have taken on a kind of spiritual authority; his deeds have become a saga of the spirit; his person has been lifted up among the Hindu gods. Not since Buddha has such a divine presence appeared. And what is true of India is true as well of all the world! While he lived, Gandhi was a controversial figure. He was seen and criticized as a politician, statesman, nationalist leader in time of crisis. But now that he is dead, he takes his place among the half-dozen supreme spiritual saviors of the race, and receives the homage of mankind. Death had not touched him, except to release an energy which is more than human, and thus divine.

Article in *Opinion*,
September–October, 1949

STEPHEN S. WISE
(1874–1949)

In a letter to John Haynes Holmes in early 1948 Stephen S. Wise addressed him as "one of the oldest and dearest of my friends." That autumn, in what was to be the last of his seventy-five years, Wise wrote a tribute for a wider audience in an editorial for Opinion, the magazine he edited. Wise, referring to the recent dedication of the new sanctuary of the Community Church, asserted: "Great preacher though Holmes be, he is far more than a preacher of matchless eloquence. He has for more than four decades been guide, friend and inspirer to all the people, irrespective of race, creed or color, and has made the Community Church the spiritual and moral abode of men, irrespective of creed or color or national origin, to all of whom he stands as a veritable apostle of faith in what God is and of what man, unshackled, may become."

Wise's high regard for Holmes had begun forty-two years before, in the spring of 1907 on the very day the two men met, as Robert Collyer introduced them at a meeting of New York's Liberal Ministers Club; and it was to remain unabated for the rest of the rabbi's life. Countless instances of this constant in his admiration of Holmes abound in the archives of Stephen Wise.

In May of 1911 Wise noted in his journal that, at the fourth anniversary dinner of the Free Synagogue, Holmes had given "a seven minute speech that was brilliant, . . . such a generous, warmhearted, and loving utterance with regard to me, and so full of the magnanimity which he always shows and feels toward me that he just won the hearts of all, who gave him a stirring welcome and a magnificent storm of applause at the close."

Even when Wise and Holmes disagreed, their extraordinary friendship remained undisturbed. The unique kinship, both intellectual and spiritual, withstood the strain. They were not of one mind, decidedly not, in both World Wars; but the friendship was unharmed even when placed under the most intense pressure. In 1917 Stephen Wise paid special tribute to Holmes and the congregation for his antiwar views and their support of his unpopular stand. By the winter of 1916–17 Wise had become an ardent supporter of the foreign policy of President Woodrow Wilson; and on April 8, 1917, the Sunday after the U. S. Congress had declared war on Germany, Wise, preaching on "The World War For Humanity," praised the President's war message as "the world's Magna Carta" in the crusade against "Hohenzollernism and Despotism, . . . a pitiless Caesarism." In the midst of Wise's plea for national unity of "a united and indivisible people fused together by a high and irresistible purpose," he saluted Holmes:

I would refer today to my pride, yea, more than pride, in the word and action of a friend, honored and cherished, the minister of the Unitarian Church of the Messiah of this city, one of the bravest and noblest preachers of our time. We are not of one mind touching this war, though for years we have been anti-militarist fellow-workers. . . . Nothing could be more splendid than his courage, unless it be the fine determination of the people of his church, even though they are not at one with him, not to suffer any denial of his freedom of utterance within their pulpit. Prussianism is become the shame and confusion of the great German people because of its insistence that all men shall think alike and speak alike, because of its insistence upon the regimentation of the intellectual and spiritual life of the people. I thank God for the consequence-scorning nobleness of a minister of religion, ready to lay down his office and to brave the frowns of the world rather than compromise with the truth as God gives it to him to see the truth. But the congregation of the Church of the Messiah matches the nobleness of its leader, for, though it does not stand with him any more than I do in nonresistant neutrality toward this war, it sets a new standard for the liberty of the pulpit to which it is the abiding distinction of John Haynes Holmes to have given a new honor and a new glory.

In January, 1928, Wise helped the magazine Unity celebrate its fiftieth anniversary by writing for its constituency a message which hailed the longtime (1880–1918) editorial direction of the journal by his friend Jenkin Lloyd Jones (b.1843 – d.1918), "one of the prophets, if prophets there still be, of liberalism and unity in religious life in America, . . . the very incarnation of the spirit of the unafraid in quest of truth," and the editorial leadership of John Haynes Holmes. In the next paragraph Wise wrote, "I shall say nothing about Jenkin Lloyd Jones' successor in the editorship of Unity, [for] I love and honor him too much to speak of him with moderation," and then he proceeded to do just the opposite of what he had promised: "He [Holmes] is a true preacher of religion. He is a mighty prophet of righteousness and he is one of the most effective social forces of our generation. I often place the editor of Unity, John Haynes Holmes, by the side of Theodore Parker. It is no little thing to say of Unity's present editor that he is equal to the traditions of Theodore Parker in his pulpit, and of Jenkin Lloyd Jones in the editorial columns of Unity."

In this vein Wise always spoke and wrote of his colleague-contemporary. In the introduction to Holmes's book of sermons in 1932, The Sensible Man's View of Religion, Wise said: ". . . Somehow the miracle of the preacher is renewed in these pages, sensitive, understanding, genuine, . . . utterly compelling as none other in the American pulpit. We have in these sermons and addresses something priceless, a fragment of an incomparably rich and significant, uniquely vivid and vibrant personality, . . . a torch bringing light as do few men in any generation, a kindling flame to multitudes who gladly sit at the feet of this prophet and feel themselves blessed." In a letter of greeting to the convention of Zeta Beta Tau fraternity in May, 1933, as Holmes accepted their Richard Gottheil Medal, Wise wrote the delegates:

> Israel has many friends, some of them occasional friends, some of them abiding friends, [but] John Haynes Holmes is so much more than a friend of Israel. Out of the clarity of his vision and out of the richness of his generosity and out of his flaming passion for justice and the right, he has come, though an Aryan of the Aryans whatever that may mean, a Gentile and a Christian, to see eye to eye with the Jewish people touching many of the problems which they face. . . . Will you not convey to my brother in aims and in arms, America's noblest preacher, America's loftiest spiritual leader, my most affectionate greetings?

No less appreciative were the phrases Wise scribbled on a piece of paper as cues for his introduction of Holmes at the thirty-first-anniversary observance of the Free Synagogue in 1938:

> Some men great in one thing—Christian relations, or Negro, or free speech, or civic life, or Palestine, or India. He great and serviceable in all. Men speak of prophetic eloquence. What is it—this divine afflatus? Seeking truth and uttering it without fear or reservation. When the rest of us succumbed, he was true in the day of war. God gave us men— a time like this demands. God has given us one man, and his name is—Johannan (Hebrew "The Lord is gracious.") The grace of God is on his speech and on his soul. The eloquence of a life. What he says—he is and does!

In 1947 when Louise Waterman Wise, the rabbi's life companion for almost half a century, passed away, Holmes was in India on a lecture tour and could do no more than cable condolences from Calcutta. In the midst of grief for the death of his wife, Wise said to his children over and over again, "If only Holmes were here, if only Holmes were here."

Fourteen months later, Wise, on his sickbed in the Lenox Hill Hospital, dictated to his secretary a farewell letter for his family, a moving document found after he had passed away on April 19, 1949. In the directions carefully outlined for his funeral service, he had noted: "I would like a prayer or the reading of a poem by my beloved friend, Holmes."

[Rabbi Stephen] Wise and I first met in the spring of 1907. . . . We came traipsing into town together—he from the West, and I from Boston. . . . The real beginning of his career was his declination, as a young rabbi in Portland, Oregon, of the tempting call to the pulpit of Temple Emanu-El [in New York City] and his swift coming to this city to found the Free Synagogue. . . . There was something about his eruption in New York, defying conventions, proclaiming freedom all anew, which shook the town and made every champion of prophetic religion straightway his friend. . . . We discovered our oneness of sentiment, our fixed conviction, that religion is here to save men from injustice and oppression, and society from sin.

. . . Our friendship began with our first meeting, and lasted until Wise's death, just short of a half-century of time. It came "out of the depths," and therefore had little to do with any identity or likeness of opinion. It was amazing, when you come to think of it, that two friends who held matters of opinion not lightly could agree to disagree on so many different points. One would think, for example, that the two World Wars which rent and pulverized our civilization would have worked havoc with even the stoutest friendship. Once, and then again, this dear relationship was bent but it never broke. Our differences were not insignificant. Wise was ardently pro-war [in 1917–18], and with his son, Jim, went into the shipyards to prove it. I was as strongly anti-war, and joined the Quakers and other extreme pacifist groups. I suppose that we saw less of one another during these periods than either before or after. But our friendship was all the more precious for the burdens that it bore.

. . . With Wise and myself it was the constant recognition of the mutuality of our work which bound and held us together. Church and synagogue were one in the light of the spirit. Lessing had long since anticipated us in his great drama, *Nathan der Weise*, when Christian and Jew join hands, and the Christian says,

Nathan, you are a Christian . . . better never lived.

to which Nathan replies,

Indeed! The very thing that makes me seem
Christian to you, makes you a Jew to me.

The relationship between Wise and myself ripened through the years and became even as the love of David and Jonathan. To explain this sentiment has been more difficult than to live it. The negative side of the experience has become plain—the fact, namely, that friendship has nothing to do with such mere externalities as opinions, ideas, modes of life, fashions of thought, whims, fancies, extravaganzas, dull conformities, routines or formulas of conduct. These are hopelessly shallow and temporal, and thus in no way fundamental. But, as to all reality, there is a positive side which reveals the mystical and therefore mysterious character of friendship. Do you ask what bound Wise and me together? I answer:

First, a passion for righteousness which was common to us

both. This passion brought us together on a hundred battle-fronts, and welded us into a single instrument of victory and defeat. This passion never cooled, never compromised, least of all surrendered. When Wise died, it was as though I had lost half or more of my spiritual being, and therewith had begun myself to die.

The second thing that held us together is as simple as it is complex. We have said most when we have said least—that Wise and I discovered early that we had not only esteem but love, one for another. True friendship, the kind that Plato, Cicero, and Emerson talked about, fulfills itself soon or late, and lifts life into splendor. It explains everything or nothing. But it is "wonderful, passing the love of woman."

Rabbi Wise [was] a great Jew. One of his noblest qualities [was] his devotion to his people. In his early years, this was a cheerful task. It is true that on the fringes of our Western life, the ghetto still lingered and the Jew was still oppressed. Anti-Semitic prejudice could still be encountered even in England and America. The Dreyfus case showed what searing flames were buried beneath cooling ashes. But the nineteenth century had brought in an era of emancipation, in which the Jew had richly shared. Indeed, assimilation was one of the problems of the hour. So the scene was bright with hope when Stephen Wise began his memorable ministry. But with the First World War came tragedy. Since then the scene . . . darkened into agony and terror, and the Jew . . . [was] cast into the blackest pit of horror that even this chosen victim of oppression has ever known. And always . . . the great Rabbi fought the good fight to save his people. He spared himself no labor, no sacrifice, no tears. Body, mind and soul, property and life itself, were laid as offerings on Israel's altar. The service of Zion was central in his labors for Israel. And I thank God for His mercy that Wise himself survived to witness the triumph of Zion's cause.

Rabbi Wise [was] a great American. It is perhaps because he was not born here, and therefore [saw] America as set against the background of the Europe in which he would have suffered and perhaps died had not his parents early escaped to these shores, that he [felt] a very especial passion of devotion to this adopted land. But loyalty [was] his very nature, and of course [was] poured forth as a libation of love for his country. His patriotism [began] with New York, of which he [was] for nearly a half-century . . . one of the most useful citizens. It would be difficult to name a movement for civic righteousness, a crusade for public decency and honor, in which he [was] not . . . a commanding and on occasion a lonely figure, again and again . . . the first to lift the cry of alarm, and, until victory [was] won, among the first to guide and animate the struggle.

But New York [was] only the beginning of his endeavor. From the time he was a young rabbi on the Pacific Coast, . . . he [was] engaged in every undertaking for the public interest. The greatest in the land . . . sought his counsel and knew his friendship; the humblest and sorely beset . . . felt his compassion and received his aid. And all because he . . . believed in America as a nation of free men, whom he would not have defeated in their quest of brotherhood. Early in his stalwart manhood, he caught the vision of democracy, and resolved that this vision should be fulfilled here, and so throughout the world. He [was] . . . sorely tried with war, corruption, and decay. Must the American dream fade and disappear? Not if his life and his labor could avail. What country has had a nobler citizen, and what faith a truer prophet?

Rabbi Wise [was] a great man. This [was] manifest in all his qualities, . . . built on heroic lines. Just to look upon his physique, in the high noon-tide of his strength and power, was to see the inward as well as the outward stature of his being. This physique would have been a peril, had it not been quickened and motivated and possessed by a soul as pure as it was brave. Which means that it was religion which transfigured him to greatness! Rabbi Wise, in other words, [was] a great man because he [was] a great spiritual force. One imagines that he would have been great in any career he might have chosen. But when he chose the synagogue, it was because he knew God, and would serve Him evermore. It is comfort to my heart that in this age of horror, God . . . found witness in this man.

Of most men, it may be said that their personalities are of a dual character. This certainly was true of Wise. Thus there was that aspect of his nature which he displayed to the world as rabbi, reformer, public leader, incomparable orator, and prophet, and which was the only side of him that most people ever saw at all. In this sense Wise may not unfairly be described as a man of the masses, a crowd man. To be at his best, he needed numbers of men and women about him, to challenge him or cheer him on.

Rabbi Wise was at his best, as an orator, when addressing great audiences. He reacted instantly to the larger audience when it appeared. Give him a crowd of five hundred or a thousand, and the speaker's effectiveness mounted. Multiply these thousands, and passion began to seize him, and to shake him like a reed in the wind, till eloquence appeared. As though by some sweeping gesture of command, Wise suddenly became relaxed and released from tensions which had bound him. He rose in stature like a man inspired, and swept his vast audience as though by some mystic hurricane let loose upon them. His massive throat muscles swelled and throbbed. The incomparable voice took on the thunders of a later Sinai. It was Moses speaking again the word of prophecy.

This outward and public aspect of Wise's nature was seen in the great parade which he led on foot through the streets of New York in 1933 in protest against the Hitler horrors in Nazi

Germany. I shall never forget that day of demonstration against iniquity. What a meeting that was [in Madison Square Garden], and what a parade! Thousands of men, women, and even children, mostly from the poorer classes, the slum-dwellers of the East Side. Most of them, in their working clothes, unwashed, yet strangely clean. Their footbeats on the pavements were keeping time—block after block. The silence echoed the lamentations that the heart alone could sing. Nor were there uniforms, unless we count the garb of the ancient rabbis, with their towering hats, their sweeping beards, their black robes trailing the ground, and here and there the scrolls of the sacred law. Of worldly banners there were none, save only the nation's flag hanging limp upon its staff, as though mourning for [the people of] Israel on this tragic day. What a multitude this was—like a great river rolling on to the sea! And at its head one solitary figure who, by his mere presence, suffused the whole with dignity and power.

There was something in Wise's appearance that day which marked him for attention. There was the mighty stride which bore him beyond the easy compass of other men to follow. There was his bared head with its black mane of hair rolling back from his noble brow. As usual, his large black felt hat was in his hand, to be lifted in response to some silent salute from the crowds of spectators on either side. Wise's clothing was unchanged—the same black suit, with its long and heavy folds in Prince Albert style which had long since become familiar. He was getting dusty as his feet tramped on, and obviously tired from this exhausting day. Even his giant-like frame could not indefinitely endure without fatigue. But he moved undaunted, and could have gone miles further had duty called. His face that day was stern and terrible. It was molded as a block of granite, and knew not a single smile.

Beside this consummate and dedicated leader I trudged

along, offering my shoes to the great cause of Israel. Outwardly I was happy at what was being done, but inwardly ashamed that there were not more Christians in line to sustain, if only for pity's sake, their Jewish brethren.

But there was another aspect of Wise's nature, the inward in contrast to the outward. It may seem incredible that Wise ever turned away from the great and general public, to that more intimate private aspect of his being. But no one who did not follow him into his home and heart, away from "the tumult and the shouting," . . . could ever know the man as he really was. Tenderness is what I would call this inner quality of being which was his—tenderness which shades off into gentleness, compassion, and in the end to that sense of pity which is so near akin to love, . . . the tenderness which was central to Wise's very life, the inward and deep secret of his being. The rabbi was at times severe, even fierce. But these moods, stirred by the bitterness of the fight against cruelty and wrong, never lasted. As in the ancient days of the Judges in the Old Testament, ". . . out from the strong came forth sweetness."

It seemed at times that Wise never would be understood in the full grandeur of his being. In the crowning years of his heroic struggle against wickedness and wicked men, he was necessarily the fighter with heroic cries upon his lips. Men feared him for his power, but worked with him because of the mighty deeds he did, and [because] in public meetings [he] drew such crowds. But it was these crowds, the common people, who understood him all along, and knew the pitying heart within which was all but smothered by the thundering storm without. It was all at last so clearly disclosed in the funeral services at Carnegie Hall [on April 22, 1949]. As I looked about me, and saw the great throng of men and women crowding that vast auditorium as a full tide fills the sea, I whispered to my soul, "They knew him for his greatness." Then the service was done, and we marched onto the rain-swept streets and saw crowds of patient witnesses, waiting, mile after mile, "through storm and flood," to pay their last honors to the dead, and again my soul whispered to itself, "These knew him and loved him for his goodness."

Articles in *Congress Weekly*, March 21, 1949, and *Aufbau*, March, 1949; introduction to *The Personal Letters of Stephen Wise*, 1956

FOR STEPHEN WISE'S SEVENTY-FIFTH BIRTHDAY

Walk firmly, brother, this is not the end;
New summits wait the coming of your feet.
Speak bravely, brother, all our ears we bend
To heed your word which never sounds retreat.

You lead us still; we follow where you tread,
Weary and worn, but quickened by your call
That, like a trumpet, scatters fear and dread,
And summons to your side your comrades all.

I ponder well the time when you were young,
And lifted high a sword of living flame;
You spoke with roll of thunder on your tongue,
And God's own angels gathered where you came.

A wrapt Isaiah again, you heard God's word,
"Whom shall I send, my purpose to fulfill?"
And straight and tall, you stood before the Lord,
And cried, "Send me, to do thy perfect will."

The years have flown, God's banner droops and dips,
And you are weary from the ceaseless fight.

But still the living coal burns on your lips,
And high the sword is pointed to the light.

We grope and falter on the road you trod;
We look to you to show us the way.
Your scars are decorations earned of God.
Your presence promises the brighter day.

1949

II

HIS CREDO

Sometimes a man puts forth upon the world,
As from a hidden place of power hurled,
A thrust of splendor from the Creative breast,
A spoken word of speed that knows no rest;
An uttered energy, a seething skill,
An arrow straight from the Eternal Will.

No timid message his, no mystic goal,
But shock and terror for the sluggish soul;
The piercing of security; the smart
Of sudden Truth embedded in the heart.
The righteous hate him and the smug would spell
Damnation for the gospel he would tell.

For Truth is terrible and gives no pause,
No compromise with her implacable laws.
And Truth would bid us hurt whom we adore,
Forsake the loved because we love her more;
Mother and child apart, father and son,
If justice through such severing be won.

Yet Love it was that sped him from the bow,
And Love it is that bids him strike the blow
That shatters dull deception, but to free
The long-imprisoned Truth for you and me.
He shakes our superstitions to the dust,
He breaks the ancient law, because he must.

Sometimes God breathes a soul into the world
As from His inmost ecstasy unfurled:
"Be utterance for Me. Be hands and feet,
Strong and intrepid as My own heart beat.
Declare My living purpose and My plan—
Breaker and builder 'bodied in one man."

—ANGELA MORGAN, "A Tribute To
John Haynes Holmes," 1926

THE QUEST

For ages we have been taught to believe that the revelation of God was once open to certain holy men of old, but that that race of holy men is now ended, the revelation of God closed, and only its memory preserved in the rites of a church or the pages of a book. For ages we have been told that God was once seen by blessed eyes, but that now he is seen no more, and can be found only in the traditions of earlier days. But now, at last, a new and better conception of God and of the revelation of His spirit is dawning upon the minds of men. We are today coming to see that God is literally He in Whom we live and move and have our being—God the life at the heart of all things—God the spirit which lights the stars by night, beats in the ocean's waves, and sings in the songs of birds—and God the spirit also which breathes in the throbbing heart of man. Would we see God, therefore, then must we endeavor to find Him as He is revealed to us day by day, hour by hour, and moment by moment, revealed in the outward phenomena of nature and revealed in the inward phenomena of the spirit. . . .

Those therefore are true prophets who have turned in upon themselves and communed with their own souls—those the true revealers of the life of God who have gazed upon the sanctuaries of their own spirits and made known what there they saw. Amos and Hosea, Micah and Isaiah, Socrates and Jesus, Buddha and Mohammed, Savonarola and Luther, Wesley and Fox, Theodore Parker and Phillips Brooks—all of these and countless others have been prophets of the soul and revealers unto men of the light and life of God. But God has had other prophets as well, and has revealed Himself not only in the secret places of the soul but also in the open places of the world. Not only the gaze inward but the gaze outward has found God's face and revealed its features unto men. . . . For in every star that walks the night, and in every flower that perfumes the day—in every wave that beats upon the shore, and in every pebble that rolls upon the beach—in every reptile and every fish, in every bird and every beast—in all is God, and they who know the secrets of these things know by that token the secrets of the life of God. . . .

These devoted learners, I know, have been regarded in all ages by the church as the destroyers of religion and have been persecuted as the enemies of God. Copernicus escaped persecution only by death. Giordano Bruno was burned alive as a monster of impiety. Galileo was imprisoned and silenced as the worst of unbelievers. Kepler was considered as one who was "throwing Christ's kingdom into confusion with his silly fancies." Newton was outlawed by the church for "dethroning Providence." But these men, like all men of their kind—the quiet students of Nature and of Nature's laws—have been not the enemies but the friends of religion. . . . They have revealed God ever more and more clearly to the souls of men—indeed have done more to reveal God than all the church's priests from Aaron to Pius X.

> Sermon, "Darwin's Contribution to
> the Doctrine of Evolution,"
> *The Messiah Pulpit*, 1909

THE INEFFABLE

God has revealed Himself in a twofold way—first, in the world of nature, and, second, in the world of men. God has revealed Himself in the first place, I say, in the physical universe—nature is itself a Bible in whose pages are revealed the secrets of God's life. His greatness is seen in the profound abyss of the sky above our heads, in the vast expanse of the earth beneath our feet, in the mighty grandeur of the ocean; His beauty is revealed in the brilliant light of the day, in the soothing darkness of the night, in the flaming procession of the stars, in the bird on speeding wings, in the flower whose fragrance and loveliness are given freely even "on the desert air"; His mercy is revealed in the majestic succession of the season, in the gentle rains that nourish the parched ground, in the fertile soil that yields its abundance of grain and fruit; His strength is revealed in the sweep of the tempest, the violence of the volcano, the throes of the earthquake. What person has ever come near to nature and not seen therein the revelation of God's spirit? Through all the physical universe there runs the all-pervading life of God—hence is every particle of this universe in itself a revelation of the Divine. There is no pebble in the soil so obscure, no flower in the field so tiny, no star in the sky so distant, that it does not reveal to us as much of God as it possesses.

In the second place, God is revealed to us in the world of men—of human experience. The history of human life here upon the planet has simply been one never-ceasing revelation of the divine life. In the soul of every man is latent the spirit of God—therefore in every uplifting thought that he thinks, in every pure emotion that he feels, in every honest word that he speaks, in every noble deed that he performs, is every man revealing God. If the thought be degrading, the emotion impure, the word dishonest, the deed ignoble, then is the guilty man misinterpreting God—betraying, not revealing Him. But just in so far as his life is pure and true, just in so far is that life God's revelation. We behold God revealed in every bond of love that binds friend to friend, husband to wife, parent to child—in every sacrifice in defense of truth and right—in every service for mankind. The higher man's thought, the nobler his emotion, the braver his word, the more devoted his deed, the clearer and truer is the revelation of God which is there manifested. In the degree, that is, that every human life approximates to the ideal of the perfect life, to that degree at least is God's spirit revealed to men. God is present in every human soul; therefore, through every human soul, in some obscurely, in some clearly, is the revelation of God shown forth. "Ineffable," says Emerson, "is the union of man and God in every act of the soul."

> Sermon, "Revelation,"
> *The Old and the New,* 1906

WHAT GOD MEANS TO ME

In the first place, God means to me Purpose. He is the Purpose which has been working in the hearts of men from the day when first man stood erect and moved from out the realm of animal existence. It seems as though the story of mankind were nothing but a story of a chaos futilely seeking some kind of order or progress. Imbedded in the complexity of human catastrophes and dreams, is design which is slowly but surely working itself out. This element of Purpose becomes most clearly manifest in the constant rise of man out of the wreckage and ruin of one convulsing cataclysm after another. What does this mean, if not that he is working out a Purpose which is greater than he himself knows?

In the second place, God means to me Will—the Will which labors unceasingly to fulfill the Purpose of which we have just been speaking. Indeed, at our highest moments, both in our individual and social lives, do we not feel as if we were caught up, as it were, by a "power not ourselves which makes for righteousness," justice and peace upon the earth? This "power not ourselves" is the Will we are doing blindly, stupidly, and yet in the end triumphantly, when we give our lives to great causes of human emancipation. What man is today is explained by the material conditions in the midst of which he has lived and struggled. But it is only explained finally when we recognize the presence of this resolute determination of the universe to achieve its ends and fulfill in man the utmost of its purposes.

Lastly, God means to me Love—Love in the working out of this Will and the achievement of this Purpose. Even in the cruel realms of animal existence, the idea of mutual service made its appearance in the early dawn of organic existence, and as the ages have moved on through the hundreds and thousands of years gone by, this principle, which at heart is none other than the principle of Love, has grown ever stronger and more decisive in its influence. In spite of all the evil and cruelty of life, Love is present within this universe, and this Love I cannot understand, either in origin or character, save as I think of it as God.

God is the Life-Spirit of the world, working unconsciously in nature and consciously in man, his Purpose, Will and Love. To many this may seem to be but a way of speaking, a deliberate and unreasonable insistence on using theistic instead of humanistic terms. To me there is something more involved here than a chosen method of intellectual interpretation. God has become to me something more than a formula for the explanation of natural and historical phenomena. God is now, to me, an experience, well nigh impossible to explain, but felt as surely as the air we breathe or the sunshine in the midst of which we live. There are moments in our lives, if we struggle ever to be faithful to the best within us, when God appears as a veritable presence—One Who speaks His words of comfort, touches our hands in strength and guidance, and gives us companionship in moments of loneliness and pain. To all of us there come times when we are lifted up, so to speak, to the doing of things which of ourselves we could never have done.

He only is the religious man who, whatever his creed or lack of creed, has touched these mystic shores of his own spiritual knowledge. By prayer, by devotion to truth, by love of our fellow-men, by rigorous discipline to simple and pure modes of life, above all by valiant consecration to every emancipating cause, we find our way to God and see Him at the last as a comrade and a friend.

Sermon, *The Community Pulpit,*
1920

THE REALITY OF PRAYER

The one thing that men need in this world to make their lives pure and strong and true is the consciousness within their souls of the ever-living God; and any prayer, however crude its phrase or childish its thought, which serves to create this consciousness within the soul is to that extent at least worth while. It is useless to think that God can be persuaded by our prayers to suspend one single law in our behalf, it is criminal to wish that He could do so; but it is only truth to say that, by our prayers, we bring ourselves into the knowledge and the love of God, and therewith gain more and better help than if suddenly every law in the universe were altered to our benefit.

The turn of one little button on the walls of my house sends the electric current coursing through every wire, and bringing light to every nook and cranny of the place. Prayer, it seems to me, is the little button by which the love of God may be diverted from the powerhouse of His spirit and carried into every remotest corner of the human heart. If the button remains untouched, the home remains in darkness; so, if prayer is never offered, the human heart is never united with the Divine Presence. But the powerhouse of God is always there, and it only remains for me—not God!—to say as to whether the eternal life, there ceaselessly being generated, shall bring its heat and light and power into my life.

Sermon, "Prayer,"
The Messiah Pulpit, 1913

PRAYER AS AN ART

In its simplest origins, as in its profoundest deeps, prayer is unutterable; but in frequent moments it seeks expression and finds a language. This language is nothing unique, strange, or superstitious. It is as natural as a child calling to its mother, or Burns to the daisy and the field mouse. It has nothing to do with theological dogma and little with religious practice, but only with poetry as the language of the soul.

I may or may not picture [God] as a personal deity, as Titian pictured him in the "Assumption" and Michelangelo in his Creation fresco. What matters is that in my feeble and perhaps curious way I am thinking of the universe, as Shelley of the skylark, that I may outsoar the confines of my earthly life. I am reaching out to an Over-Soul, as Wordsworth to the buried and yet immortal soul of Milton, that I may find strength greater than my own to serve the world, all in the conviction that in the vast realm of being, there is a spirit akin to man, and that the two may meet in mutual accord and be of mutual assistance.

Prayer is not the practice of magic in the hope of miracle. Rather is it the exercise of religion in the quest of "ideal ends."

If it moves from psychology to theology, it is because man must rationalize his impulses. If it transforms desire into action, it is because man must realize and not merely contemplate his purposes. If it seeks expression in poetic speech, it is because man must have communion with his larger self. Prayer is as natural as it is lovely, and as effective as it is spontaneous. What prayer might do, if dedicated to great instead of petty ends, and if disciplined by sure mastery of the spirit, no man dare estimate. But all through history there run the intimations of this strange power. Today, in the experimentations of psychology and the trained practices of religion, there appears the beginning at least of an art, or craft, of the inner life. Not distant may be the day when prayer will be everywhere recognized as a necessary, beneficent and lovely part of the culture of the race.

Rethinking Religion, 1938

THE BIBLE: HINDRANCE OR HELP?

May I state how utterly mistaken I think it is for anybody to argue seriously that the Bible should be cast aside altogether, as no longer of service to the aims and purposes of modern religion? Whenever this sweeping indictment is put before me for consideration, I find myself picking up a copy of this ancient volume of spiritual lore, and scanning with fresh interest its contents.

Here in the beginning are the folk tales of old Israel—as precious a treasure of legend and tradition as those passed down to us, and long since accepted at their true value, from Greece and Rome. Then comes, in the books of Judges, Samuel, and Kings, the story of Hebrew history—a story of incalculable worth as the narrative of a people preeminent in their apprehension of things moral and spiritual, and relentless in their pursuit of the divine. What the Athenians did for us in literature and art, what the Romans did for us in legislation and social order, this the Hebrews did for us in religion, and here in these ancient books is the only first-hand story we have of their endeavors, failures and successes in this most sacred of all realms of racial experience.

Next I turn the pages of Job—a poem of such titanic proportions from the standpoint both of thought and expression, that it can be compared with nothing less than the *Iliad* of Homer, the *Aeneid* of Virgil, and the *Divine Comedy* of Dante. Then appear the Psalms, the great hymn book of the temple of old Israel. Here is the Twenty-third Psalm ("The Lord is my shepherd"), an immortal chant of life and death; the 104th ("Bless the Lord, O my soul"), a nature song unrivaled for power and beauty; and the 139th ("O Lord, thou hast searched me and known me"), the supreme religious poem of all the ages.

And here are the Prophets—Amos, Hosea, Isaiah, Jeremiah, and the rest—those mighty men of God who taught the law of righteousness, formulated the principles of social justice, and dreamed their dreams of the coming of that great day of the Lord when every man shall dwell under his own vine and fig tree, when nation shall not lift up sword against nation, neither learn war any more, when old wastes shall be builded, former desolations raised up, and all men everywhere released from misery and death.

From the Old Testament I pass over to the New, and meet at once the majestic figure of the Nazarene. I hear his Sermon on the Mount, his parables, his two commandments of the law; I see his love of the common people, and his service of their need; I catch his vision of that Kingdom of God, which shall bring "peace on earth, goodwill to men." Then I pass to the hero tales of Paul and the Apostles—martyrs to an age which knew not the secret of their word. And lastly I dwell for one radiant moment with John on Patmos, and behold with him "the holy city, new Jerusalem, coming down out of heaven from God, made ready as a bride adorned for her husband."

This is the Bible, as I know it in my work. And this is the Bible I am told must be thrown away as a hindrance and not a help to modern religion! How extravagant a claim, and how irreparable a loss is threatened by this claim! It is impossible to conceive what the religion of the past would have been without this book, just as it is impossible to conceive how the religion of the present could dispense with its inspiration, and whither the religion of the future would tend without its guidance. I assume, of course, that in the last analysis the Bible is no more indispensable than any other transcendent religious literature. We all agree that at bottom this volume has been created by the spirit of man, and that this spirit therefore is itself the original and permanent reality. Without this volume, the spirit of man could still live and still find communion with its God. Nay, more, it could write another and as good a Bible. Destroy every word of the Bible, said Emerson, in one of his self-reliant moods, and I will write it anew! Religion, after all, would not only survive, but flourish still in fragrance and great beauty, if the Bible were deliberately and wholly cast aside. But the loss would be none the less great, and the injury to religion serious. Free as I want to be, as I must insist upon being, from all fetters of traditionalism, I still find it difficult to conceive how we could carry on our religious work with effectiveness and ease, if we were denied the use of the Hebrew and Christian Scriptures. What elevation is given to our expression of spiritual devotion by the noble cadences of these ancient Psalms! What authority is added to our appeal for the establishment of new standards of social justice, by the triumphant leadership of the Prophets! How compelling becomes our vision of human brotherhood, when linked with the teachings and example of the carpenter of Nazareth!

There is nothing temporary or passing in these documents.
They are the testimony not of a single age, or race, or personality. In them speaks the soul of the whole to all peoples and
to all times. They are the spirit bearing witness of itself, and
therewith voicing eternity.

> Sermon, "Is the Bible a Hindrance
> or a Help to Modern Religion?,"
> *The Messiah Pulpit*, 1917

THE CHRIST OF DOGMA VERSUS
THE JESUS OF HISTORY

The spirit of our time—the spirit of reform, of social change,
of "a new heaven and a new earth"—is the spirit which is
matched not by the divine Christ but by the human Jesus. Just
as the Christ of Dogma is centered in the life to come, so the
Jesus of History is centered in the life that now is. He alone
can help us in this great task of rebuilding the world after the
pattern of justice and of peace; and he can help us, as can no
other man who has ever lived. For he it was who dreamed of
the Kingdom of God, an ideal society which should some day
be established on the earth. He it was who, if he did not actually
discover the laws of this ideal society, at least formulated them
in such perfect form, that the love which shall save the world
is identified forever with his name. Above all it was he who
lived the Kingdom in his own heart, and died for the sake of
transmitting it to the hearts of other men.

Do we want to see the world which we must build out of the
wreck and ruin of our day? Then must we acquaint ourselves
with the mind of the Nazarene. Do we want to find the spirit
in which we must work to this end? Then must we learn the
precepts of the carpenter-prophet. The Christ of Dogma cannot

help us in this work. The Incarnate Lord is distant far from all these commonplace duties of social reconstruction. But the Nazarene who knew the ways of Palestine, talked with fishermen and shepherds, and by his revolutionary gospel shook state and church to their foundations, may lead us, if we will follow. In the Jesus of History, and in none other, is "the way, the truth, and life."

To put to one side the Christ of dogma is to lose nothing but superstitions which have done their work and served their day. To take to one's soul the Jesus of history is to gain everything that human annals have to offer in terms of spiritual idealism.

The exchange is all to the good and cannot be made too soon. For long enough has the mighty Nazarene, as Christ the Lord, been the sport of theologians, the pride of priests, the sword of kings. Time is it, high time, that he became at last today, as he was yesterday, a man who loved men, one of the common people, that in and through his own, he may still labor for his Kingdom.

Sermon, *The Messiah Pulpit*, 1917

JESUS A THEOLOGIAN?

Jesus knew nothing of the dogmas of the Christian creeds—the fall of man, the inheritance of sin, damnation as a punishment for sin, the incarnation, the atonement, salvation, and redemption—and would not have understood their meaning or even recognized their words. He would have looked upon the Apostle's Creed and the Athanasian Creed as having been created by minds thrown into confusion and dismay . . . As for the Westminster Confession, his sensitive spirit would be horrified by one of the most abominable statements of theology ever conceived by the mind of man.

It cannot be emphasized too often that Jesus was not a theologian. He interpreted religion as something not primarily to be believed but to be lived.

The Sensible Man's View of Religion, 1932

FORGOTTEN CHRISTS

I never ponder upon [the] accidental survival of Jesus' memory but what I find myself wondering as to the number of men who may have lived and died as Jesus lived and died, and altogether missed the good fortune of his survival in the minds of later generations. Believing as I do that Jesus was simply a man, equipped with no personal power and guided by no divine intervention denied to other men, why should I not believe that thousands of men have lived as purely and heroically as he lived, and yet been forgotten as the vast multitudes of men are destined to be forgotten always? Are there not thousands of Christs, perhaps, who have lived their lives upon this earth only to pass forever into the black darkness of oblivion?

I find myself thinking of Thomas Gray, the great English poet, and his meditations in the churchyard at Stoke Poges. You remember how he embodied his meditations in that most familiar of all English poems, "An Elegy Written in a Country Churchyard":

Perhaps in this neglected spot is laid
Some heart once pregnant with celestial fire;
Hands that the rod of empire might have sway'd,
Or waked to ecstasy the living lyre. . . .

Full many a gem of purest ray serene
The dark unfathom'd caves of ocean bear;

Full many a flower is born to blush unseen,
And waste its sweetness on the desert air.

In the next stanza, Thomas Gray names some of those forgotten geniuses who may have been sleeping beneath the sod
of the country churchyard. He speaks of some Hampton, "some
mute inglorious Milton," some greater Cromwell.

To these names may I not add the name of Christ, for in
that churchyard might well have been sleeping some spiritual
genius who saw as Jesus saw things of God, and lived in his
humble way for the coming of God's Kingdom? Christ is not
one man but many men. I believe that in all ages the Christs
have been with us, have done their work, and then passed on,
leaving behind some things for our redemption, no doubt, but
unattached to any name that can give them identification. . . .

Jesus was not unique. He was only one of the great multitude
of noble men and saintly women who have glorified the soul
of man. Jesus was not *the* Christ, but rather one of the many
Christs of history. . . .

Christianity, the religion of Jesus, is not unique. It is only
one expression of that universal spiritual idealism which constitutes the one religion of mankind. Christianity, like Jesus,
and Jesus, like Christianity, are rays flowing from a central sun
which is the life of God at the heart of all this universe. . . .

Religion is to be regarded as a universal experience of man,
which rises in the greatest souls to that perfect vision of God
whose name is love and whose will is peace. This experience is
like the tides of the sea—it mounts high in a few great places,
but it also flows far into every remotest inlet and bay. It is the
possession, in other words, of us all. We are all, in the measure
of our faith, the Christs of God. God is in us as he was in
Christ Jesus, to work his perfect will and way after the example
of the Christ, and to glorify that will and way forever.

Sermon, *The Community Pulpit*,
1928

WHAT IS CHRISTMAS?

Christmas is not so much a day as it is a custom. It begins, of course, with a day—a specific item on the calendar. But what is remarkable about it is the habit of our lives during this brief period of time. For a few hours we are transformed, transfigured, as though the spirit of God were with us.

Christmas is the time when we find it "more blessed to give than to receive"—when we gladden our lives by blessing the lives of others.

Christmas is the time when we seek to make children happy, and ourselves become as little children in innocence and purity of heart.

Christmas is the time when we hang wreaths and light candles in the windows of our homes, to give hospitable greeting to strangers who may be passing by.

Christmas is the time when we ring chimes of bells in towers and steeples, that melody may flood the skies, and overflow into the hearts of all who hear.

Christmas is the time when we band together in choirs and sing carols in the streets, that men may be reminded of the night when angels sang from heaven of "peace on earth."

Christmas is the time when wars are for a few happy hours forgotten, and men for these same few hours disarm in trust and love, as on that first Christmas when, says Milton, in his "Ode on the Morning of Christ's Nativity":

No war, or battle's sound
Was heard the world around,
The idle spear and shield were high up hung;
The hookèd chariot stood
Unstain'd with hostile blood,
The trumpet spake not to the armèd throng,
And kings sate still with awful eye,
As if they surely knew their sovran Lord was by.

The wonderful thing about Christmas is that it fulfills our dreams. It suspends our indifferences and selfishness and fears and hates, and makes men for an instant spiritually kin. No man must be hungry or homeless on this day, no child forlorn, no heart forsaken, no race despised, no nation outlawed. We must be brothers all, as children all of the one Father, and must dwell together in his Kingdom. And the Kingdom comes on Christmas day in millions of human souls the world around, so that we see the glory ere it fades again "into the light of common day."

> Christmas is the demonstration that
> All we have willed or hoped or dreamed of good
> Shall exist, not its semblance, but itself.

It is the proof that no hope is vain—that the highest vision may be made real. It is as though a spell were cast upon us, to save us for the instant from our cruelties and lusts, and make us ministers of love. The spell is fleeting—it passes quickly. But this one day, it may be caught, by the spiritual conjuration of our hearts, and be made real forever.

This is our task—to seize and hold and perpetuate the Christmastide. To love a life, and not merely a single day or season, which is delivered of prejudice and pride, hostility and hate, and committed to understanding, compassion, and goodwill! Then will there be no more Christian and pagan, Jew and Gentile, black and white, native and alien, or any other division, but only the human family, one as God is one, and heirs of His Kingdom.

Editorial in *World Alliance News*
Letter, December, 1945

EVOLUTION AND RELIGION

Evolution is today . . . a truth as clearly demonstrated as gravitation or the revolution of the earth about the sun; and if the church is not to lose the respect and allegiance of all intelligent men, it must accept this truth and remake its theology accordingly. . . .

The church at first opposed and denounced evolution because it did not understand it, and feared, as indeed at one time it seemed probable, that evolution meant the banishment of God and the annihilation of all religion as an empty and foolish superstition. But now that we have come to understand what evolution really is, and what bearing it actually has upon the development of religious thought, we are beginning to see that, while it has utterly destroyed the old theology which had to do with God as creator, the world as a creation, man as a fallen being, and Christ as an atoning redeemer, it has, in place of this old and untrue and immoral theology of the centuries, planted a new theology. . . . And, establishing this new and better and truer theology, evolution has not banished religion from men's souls, but, for the first time in human history, placed it upon an immovable foundation of rational and moral reality. . . .

In its half-century battle, therefore, against evolution, the church has been struggling against its own best friend. In this struggle against evolutionary science—as in all its struggles against all science in the past—the church has been seeking to overthrow that which had come not to destroy but to fulfill, not to injure but to save. It has been making the mistake of Jacob in the desert. Do you recall how the Old Testament tells us how Jacob met in the desert of Palestine, one night, a stranger whom in the darkness he mistook for an enemy? Fearing for his life, Jacob grappled with the unknown, and wrestled with him, seeking to overcome and slay him. All night long the two struggled back and forth in deadly combat—until at last the morning broke in the eastern skies. And with the waxing light of day, Jacob looked upon the face of his enemy, and lo, he discovered to his dismay that unwittingly he had been wrestling with an angel of God, who had come into the desert to give him succor. And Jacob, says the record, called that place Peniel, which means "the face of God"—for, said Jacob, "I have seen God face to face and my life is preserved." So with the church in its half-century struggle with evolution. The light of reason is rising athwart the skies, and lo, the church is discovering that this science, which it mistook for a foe come to devour and destroy, is in reality an angel of God. And the church, like Jacob, may well call this era of the combat against evolution Peniel—for, like Jacob, the church may say, "I have seen God face to face, and my life is preserved."

Sermon, "Is Evolution True?,"
The Messiah Pulpit, 1909

A MODERN FAITH

All I know, all I want to know is that I have found in my relations with my fellow men and in my glad beholding of the universe a reality of truth, goodness and beauty, and that I am trying to make my life as best I can a dedication to this reality. When I am in the thinking mood, I try to be rigorously rational, and thus not to go one step farther in my thoughts and language than my reason can take me. I then become uncertain as to whether I or any man can assert much about God, and fall back content into the mood of Job. When, however, in preaching or in prayer, in some high moment of inner communion or of profound experience with life among my fellows, I feel the pulse of emotion suddenly beating in my heart, and

I am lifted up as though upon some sweeping tide that is more than the sluggish current of my days, I find it easy to speak as the poets speak, and cry, as so many of them cry, to God.

But when I say "God," it is poetry and not theology. Nothing that any theologian ever wrote about God has helped me much, but everything that poets have written about flowers, and birds, and skies, and seas, and the saviors of the race, and God—whoever He may be—has at one time or another reached my soul! More and more, as I grow older, I live in the lovely thought of these seers and prophets. The theologians gather dust upon the shelves of my library, but the poets are stained with my fingers and blotted with my tears. I never seem so near truth as when I care not what I think or believe, but only with these masters of inner vision would live forever.

Essay in *The Beacon Song and Service Book*, 1935

RELIGION AS A SUPERSTITION

Take this charge that religion is a superstition! This is at least true to the extent that religion, if not a superstition, is, or has been, superstitious. Religion certainly was superstitious in its recognition of the supernatural, as was every other human interest or institution which flourished in the ages when supernaturalism was the dominant philosophy of life. The church in its doctrine of the infallibility of the Pope was superstitious, but not more so than the state in its doctrine of the divine right of the king. . . . There is superstition in religion, as there is superstition everywhere, since superstition belongs to human nature as an inevitable product of ignorance, credulity, and fear.

It may be said that religion is as superstitious as the believer who accepts it, or the age which knows it. Religion takes color from both. If medieval theologians believed that the earth was stationary and the center of the cosmos, that the seven planets moved around in oblique courses from left to right, that the outer heaven of the stars was composed not of matter but of a divine ether, and that all the machinery of the spheres was moved by a Godhead which was immovable and yet the source of motion, this was not because they were theologians, but only because they were medievalists who had taken over their science from the ancients. . . . If religion originated among the myths and legends of primitive days, and for centuries did its thinking in terms of this material, it is no more strange a fact than that astronomy had its beginning in the esoteric speculations of the ancient Chaldean astrologers, or that chemistry sprang from the weird wonders of the alchemy of the Middle Ages, and means as little that it is a superstition. Astronomy and chemistry did not so much escape from astrology and alchemy as develop out of them—just as religion is now developing out of mythology. . . . But astronomy and chemistry are none the less true sciences, and religion a sound aspect of experience.

. . . Religion, in other words, is no better than the age which produces it. It must be as superstitious and as rational, as learned and as ignorant, as enlightened and as reactionary, as civilized and as uncivilized, as the people who profess it. Religion may be described as a mirror in which the spiritual, and to a large extent the intellectual, character of an era is reflected and therefore seen. There will be superstition in religion as long as there is superstition in the world. But to assert that religion is superstition is itself a superstition. More superstitious than the man who believes that Joshua stopped the sun, or that the big fish swallowed Jonah, is the man who believes that the reverence, aspiration, dedication, and sacrifice of the human spirit, its trust in God and its surrender to His will are nothing but the empty delusions of a deceived imagination.

Rethinking Religion, 1938

RELIGION

[Religion is] a mysterious and mystic impulse working within us to make us greater than we are, and the world through us better than it is; to lift us to levels above the low ranges of physical appetite and satisfaction; to drive us to goals beyond the prudential bounds of time and sense. Religion belongs distinctively to man not because he can think and speculate, build churches and rear altars, but rather because he can sense the whole of life, catch a vision of the ideal in things real, and is willing to give his life to fulfilling this vision among men. To be compelled to serve an ideal cause by a conviction of its enduring value not merely for ourselves but for humanity and its high destiny upon earth—this is religion.

Religion appears whenever and wherever men appear who live under the compulsion of the spirit.

Rethinking Religion, 1938

MYSTICISM: THE WELLSPRING OF RELIGION

Mysticism means to me the belief in and practice of direct communion with God.

Mystics have appeared in all ages and among all peoples. They have endured ecstasies of rapture—seen visions and dreamed dreams which have lifted their souls to far-flung spaces of the soul. . . . Their words have sprung from their own inmost beings, and therewith have had a distinction of character which is unique. . . . If ancient mystics, like modern mystics, speak the same language, have the same experience, uncover the same depths of spiritual wisdom, it is not because they were in touch with one another and compared what they saw and heard as modern research workers compare experimental data. . . . They were men who dwelt apart and sank deep within themselves, and were content with the witness of their own souls. Their identity springs from the fact that they drank from the same wellsprings of the spirit, unveiled the same light of truth, sought and found, within them and above, the same consciousness of God. They laid hold on the same oneness of reality and were themselves made one.

. . . The mystics are to be believed. . . . The mystics bring in various guises a testimony of God, the soul, and immortality which is unimpeachable. They give an authority to conscience and the moral law which is absolute. After the theologians have argued their way through to reasoned propositions of the mind which, however impressive, are never conclusive, there come these mystics with their direct encounter with Truth. Like "the pure in heart [who] see God," their word is final.

. . . The mystics appear and offer their testimony, which is that of experience rather than of thought. They report what has become a part of their very lives. They describe, with frequently faltering but always rapturous tongue, what they have beheld as they behold the sun, breathed as they breathe the atmosphere, felt as they feel the beating of the blood stream in their hearts. . . . No longer bound to earth with its trammels of pure and practical reason, they have taken wings and soared aloft into the vast empyrean of immediate apprehension. Their material is now the substance of dreams and visions. It is the invisible suddenly seen with an ineffable intensity of beauty. It is the temporal transfigured into the eternal, and become truth manifest. . . . Poets and mystics alike speak with authority. For they have looked, at first "with holy dread" and then with "deep delight," upon the ultimate, and told us that it is so.

. . . In mysticism, therefore, do we find the highest and truest expression of spiritual faith, . . . a river of living water flowing to the vast ocean of eternal being and fructifying all the country through which it moves. Yet just because it is a river unchecked and unguided in its course, it needs to be guarded from pollution, or from breaking into some wild flood which inundates and therewith destroys the landscape. Mysticism, in other words, has its deadly perils:

(1) Thus, [mysticism] is constantly in danger of misunderstanding reason and displacing it from its necessary controls of life. . . . At first sight, it seems as though rationalism and mysticism were inherently opposed to one another. The one appears to be a form of bondage, the other pure freedom. The former is so indirect, even remote, in its approach to life, the latter so direct and thus immediate in its identification with life! Reason bears fetters which bind it to earth, while the soul takes wings and soars aloft.

. . . These two attributes of man's being are not contradictory, but complementary. Certainly mysticism is as unsafe as an unbridled horse if it abandons reason. More than any other activity of life, it needs and should cry out for the control and guidance of the mind. The bane of mysticism is fanaticism, even madness. . . . No wonder that mysticism has again and again forfeited the confidence of sensible men. Its extravagances are beyond all reason. . . . Reason and rapture need one another, the latter to drive and lift, the former to control and guide. Mysticism, in other words, must be rational, and therefore dwell with reason as the handmaiden of the spirit.

(2) A second danger is what Whitehead calls solitariness. The mystic seeks to be alone—naturally so, since it is not in society but in solitude that he can commune with the secrets of his own being. . . .

But there is danger in this practice of retirement. . . . Aloneness becomes an escape from the demands and the duties of existence. The mystic flees to mountain and desert in the beginning to commune with God and therewith restore his soul. Then, like the creeping inroads of a disease, idleness becomes pleasant, silence soothing, and the world's exactions happily remote. Thus, step by step, a good life becomes a sterile life, and bitterness as of brackish water the poison of the soul. What is necessary, of course, is a balance in these relations. There must be a dual contact with God and man, a moving easily and regularly from one to the other, making them to be in the end a unity of experience. . . .

(3) Lastly, there is the danger of regarding contemplation as the whole of life. To commune with one's own soul, or with nature in her lovelier moods, and therewith to find God and to know his truth—this, according to the mystic, is to live. But to what end?—this is the final question. For life can justify itself, in the last analysis, only in self-forgetting action. Thus, contemplation, or inner spiritual communion, cannot be practiced for its own sake. As a generator of power, it must have an outlet. And what can this outlet be but power for use on behalf of men in their struggle for righteousness and peace. . . .

Mysticism, in its true estate, is spiritual experience. It is therefore the beating heart of religion. Reason at its best is the interpretation and formulation of this spiritual experience. Its product is theology. Theology, like metaphysics, has its uses. One of these uses is not to serve as a substitute for religion. Yet the churches have persistently made this substitution and thereby wrought great ill.

There are many programs for the recovery of the churches. One assuredly is the rediscovery of mysticism. To supplant the theologian with the true mystic would save religion.

Essay in symposium, *Mysticism and
the Modern Mind*, 1959

THE UNDYING FIRE OF THE DIVINE

Valiant is the heart of man. Set in a world whose bounds he cannot trace—armed with puny hands and brain, to do battle against the gigantic forces of sky and sea and earth—beset behind and before by the twin mysteries of birth and death—knowing only the unknowable, searching only the unsearchable, living only to die—man has stood erect as one lifted by God's hand, and has moved ever onward, through centuries of unspeakable pain, fear and frustration, with unconquerable courage and unquenchable faith. It is impossible to read however imperfect a record of man's thoughts on death and after, as written from earliest to latest times, without confessing that there is indeed an undying fire of the divine within us, and bowing in adoration before it. Especially is this true of the testimony which has been coming to us from brave young hearts, in the filth of the trenches, in the icy wastes of the sea, even in the vast spaces of the air, during these years of the world's blackest tragedy and most awful agony. Something there is within man or above him, that makes him greater than himself, stronger than the universe, mightier than the mysteries which always challenge, and sometimes beat him downward, to despair. Man, in his fronting of death and his dream of immortality, is all that we need, after all, to teach us of God. The soul is its own best testimony to the everlasting reality of religion.

The Grail of Life, 1919

ONENESS OF ALL RELIGIONS

Humanity, for all its endless and tragic divisions into tribes and clans and nations and races, is still "of one blood," so religion, for all its divisions into churches and cults and denominations and competitive world faiths, is still of one spirit.

In the oneness of religion, we see the truth of religions. If there is to be distinction between these many religions of many peoples, it must be upon the basis not of true and false, but of high and low. For while all religions are true in the measure of their spiritual faith, yet some religions are undoubtedly higher than others in their expression of this faith. Corruption works its havoc, ignorance spreads its blight, persecution spawns its bigotry and hate. Few religions are pure, or remain pure, except as they are made pure by the lives of those who live them.

All religions are true in the measure of their fidelity to the inner spirit of man, and all religions false in the measure of their betrayal of this spirit. Or, abandoning this distinction, may we not say that all religions are true for those who profess and practice them "in spirit and in truth"?

Rethinking Religion, 1938

THE UNIVERSAL FAITH

All the religions of the world, therefore—from the most primitive to the most complex, from the most degraded to the most sublime—are from the standpoint of evolution but different manifestations of the one universal religion. All churches, from the rude shrine of the naked Zulu to the gorgeous mosque of the Moslem, from the bloody temple of the Aztec to the proud cathedral of the Christian, are but different branches of the one universal church. All prophets, from the medicine-man of the North American Indians to the gentle Buddha, from the howling dervish to the transfigured Christ, are but differently chosen messengers of the one universal Father. God revealed himself to no one chosen people, but to humanity.

From this point of view, there is no religion which is absolutely false, just as there is no art or literature or music which is wholly true or wholly false. All religions are seen to be a mixture of truth and error; all are a more or less imperfect reflection of the Infinite and the Eternal; all are in process of development from the crude and extravagant beginnings of primitive times to the lofty moral and spiritual idealism of the few great faiths of civilized humanity.

From this standpoint, all things become divine, all things secular become sacred, all truth becomes revelation; all men, be they black or white, Jew or Gentile, pagan or Christian, become the sons of the one universal Father, and all religion, whether found in ancient or modern times, among a savage or a civilized people, becomes an everlasting and universal reality.

> Sermon, "Evolution and the Problem of Revealed or Natural Religion," *The Messiah Pulpit*, 1909

IS DEATH THE END?

The final and perfect justification of our hope [in immortality], after all, must rest upon our belief in God and the soul. If these are true—and who will assert that they are not?—then it is surely something more than probable that death is not the end. The idea of immortality, in other words, is as instinctive as religion. If anything is clearer, it is that man's consciousness of God, his soul, immortal life, his persistent endeavor to verify this consciousness and answer the problems which it has raised, and his development and utilization of spiritual faculties as means of adjustment to the invisible realm revealed by this consciousness, are themselves the only verification that we need of "the everlasting reality of religion."

Man exists for something beyond this present world! Living

under the impulse of forces and to the pursuit of ends which have no permanent, or even natural, relation to this present realm of time and space, he must be destined to some farther realm where these forces and ends may find a resolution, as in a chord of music, which completes the stress and strain of long-sustained disharmonies.

. . . The immortal hope [is] the logic of the cosmic process. Our faith in the survival of man's soul fits the universe in the sense that it saves it from irrationality. Evolution, as the method of life upon this planet, is not a madness inconsistent with its own system of harmonious order, but a motive, or purpose, directed to an end. The immortal soul—this is the goal of evolution. The imperishable spirit, sprung by some miracle of transmutation from the flesh, as the organic has sprung from the inorganic and the animate from the inanimate—this is the answer to the cosmic riddle. The more thoroughly the evolutionary process is understood, the more certain it becomes that the universe has been laboring to the production of a reality that will survive and fulfill itself. Or, to pass from scientific to philosophical terms, that the universe is spirit, and man the earthly counterpart of the Eternal which is God!

Is Death the End?, 1915:
The Affirmation of Immortality, 1947

III

THE PACIFIST

Department of Church History
Rochester Theological Seminary
Rochester, New York

April 24, 1916

The Reverend John Haynes Holmes
New York City

DEAR FRIEND AND COMRADE,—

Will you tell me what your attitude will be if we go to war? I am isolated here and feel the need of touch with men who are Christians and unafraid. . . .

I fear the demand for an unconditional surrender of personal conviction will be very intolerant. . . . The war party will get control of the government, and then damn all who do not identify *it* with the flag and the genius of America.

Faithfully yours,
WALTER RAUSCHENBUSCH

IS WAR EVER JUSTIFIABLE?

From every point of view—from the standpoint of things spiritual as well as of things material, from the standpoint of the future as well as of the present—war is the antithesis of life. Its one end is to destroy what has been builded up through many years by the sweat and tears of men. Its one aim is to kill the lives which men have conceived in joy, women borne in agony, and both together reared in love. Its one supreme triumph is to turn a busy factory into a pile of wreckage, a fertile field into a desert, a home of joy into an ash-heap of sorrow, a living soul into a rotting carcass. Why, if war could once be carried through to its logical conclusions—if there were not a limit to all strength, and a point of exhaustion for every passion—mankind would long since have annihilated itself and this planet become as tenantless as the silent moon! And yet there are some—yea, there are many!—who are ready to assert that this foul business is sometimes and somewheres justifiable. This I deny without qualification or evasion of any kind. War is never justifiable at any time or under any circumstances. No man is wise enough, no nation is important enough, no human interest is precious enough, to justify the wholesale destruction and murder which constitute the essence of war. Human life is alone sacred. The interests of human life are alone sovereign. War, as we have now seen, is the enemy of life and all its interests. Therefore, in the name of life and for the sake of life, do I declare to you that war must be condemned universally and unconditionally.

Sermon, *The Messiah Pulpit*, 1915

THE GOD OF BATTLES

The remarkable thing about the religion of war is the fact that this so-called religion exactly reverses all the precepts of right and wrong which have come to man from the universal conscience of the race or from the central mind and will of God, and lays upon his startled soul the grim command to make evil henceforward his good. The ethical code of the soldier, that is to say, is the precise opposite of the ordinary ethical code of the ordinary man under ordinary conditions. It is the soldier's duty to steal—steal and destroy anything that belongs to the enemy and can serve in any conceivable way the interests of the enemy. It is the soldier's duty to bear false witness—to tell a lie on every occasion when the enemy may be deceived and thereby led astray. It is the soldier's duty to kill—to commit murder by wholesale for the destruction of the enemy and the furtherance of his own cause. These dreadful crimes, be it noted, are not laid upon the soldier as possibilities, or alternatives, or examples of better or worse. They are commands, imperatives, duties—obligations as insistent as any of the ten tables of the law. The soldier must be a thief, a liar, a murderer, else he is not a soldier. These are the laws of war, as the other and more beneficent laws of peace—and these laws must be obeyed as truly in the one case as in the other. The God of Battles, in other words, is a God who is served by deceit, violence, dishonor, cruelty, lust, murder. All of which means he is not God at all, but the Devil.

Sermon, *The Messiah Pulpit,* 1915

THE "STATEMENT TO MY PEOPLE ON THE EVE OF WAR"

It would be folly, even actual falsehood, for me to declare that I was not afraid that Sunday morning [April 1, 1917]. The truth is I was scared when I opened the door leading into my pulpit, and still more scared when I saw the throng which had gathered to hear me. . . . The mere size of the gathering was an inspiration to a preacher who, as a fighting radical, was not exactly used to overflowing congregations. . . . It all seemed like some mob scene from the theater, except that there were an awe and reverence which belonged only to the church. . . . While the congregation was engaged in singing the second hymn in the service, I quickly left the pulpit, and took my place behind the lectern on the lower level. I did this innocently enough, yet definitely, to indicate by sign and symbol that I was not preaching in routine fashion to a congregation, but rather conferring informally with my people, on an equal level of thought and feeling, to lay hold on truth where she may be found—in the hearts of men. . . .

Never, either before or since, have I felt such a hushed expectancy as came sweeping up to me, like tides out of the sea, when the hymn was done, and the people sat to hear my message. In that ineffable moment of swift silence, the holy spirit was abroad as though on wings,

> . . . drawing nigh and nigher,
> Until the lengthening wings break into fire
> At either curved point.

Reminding my congregation of the impending entrance of America into the war against Germany, I insisted on my right, indeed my duty, to speak out in expression of my views:

"War is an open and utter violation of Christianity. If war

is right, then Christianity is wrong, false, a lie. If Christianity is right, then war is wrong, false, a lie. . . .

"In its ultimate causes, this war is the natural product and expression of our un-Christian civilization. Its armed men are grown from the dragon's teeth of secret diplomacy, imperialistic ambition, dynastic pride, greedy commercialism, economic exploitation at home and abroad. In the sowing of these teeth, America has had her part; and it is therefore only proper, perhaps, that she should have her part also in the reaping of this dreadful harvest. In its more immediate causes, this war is the direst result of unwarrantable, cruel, but none the less inevitable interferences with our commercial relations with one group of the belligerents. Our participation in the war, therefore, like the war itself, is political and economic, not ethical, in its character. Any honor, dignity, or beauty which there may be in our impending action, is to be found in the impulses, pure and undefiled, which are actuating many patriotic hearts today, and not at all in the real facts of the situation. The war itself is wrong. Its prosecution will be a crime. There is not a question raised, an issue involved, a cause at stake, which is worth the life of one blue-jacket on the sea or one khaki-coat in the trenches. I question the sincerity of no man who supports this war—I salute the devotion of every man who proposes to sustain it with his money or his blood. But I say to you that when, years hence, the whole of this story has been told, it will be found that we have been tragically deceived, and all our sacrifices been made in vain. . . .

"In time of war as in time of peace, in the hour of sin as in the hour of glory, I shall love my country and serve her to the end. Nothing that she can do will end my affection or sever my allegiance. . . .

"And how shall I, a pacifist, serve my country in time of war?

"When hostilities begin, it is universally assumed that there is but a single service which a loyal citizen can render to the state—that of bearing arms and killing the enemy. Will you understand me if I say, humbly and regretfully, that this I cannot, and will not, do? If any man or boy in this church answers the call to arms, I shall bless him as he marches to the front. When he lies in the trenches, or watches on the lonely sentinel post, or fights in the charge, I shall follow him with my prayers. If he is brought back dead from hospital or battle-field, I shall bury him with all the honors not of war but of religion. He will have obeyed his conscience and thus performed his whole duty as a man.

"But I also have a conscience, and that conscience I also must obey. When, therefore, there comes a call for volunteers, I shall have to refuse to heed. When there is an enrollment of citizens for military purposes, I shall have to refuse to register. When, or if, the system of conscription is adopted, I shall have to decline to serve. If this means a fine, I will pay my fine. If this means imprisonment, I will serve my term. If this means persecution, I will carry my cross. No order of president or governor, no law of nation or state, no loss of reputation, free-dom of life, will persuade me or force me to this business of killing. On this issue, for me at least, there is 'no compromise.' Mistaken, foolish, fanatical, I may be; I will not deny the charge. But false to my own soul I will not be. Therefore here I stand. God help me! I cannot do other!

"And this resolution applies, let me now be careful to state, quite as much to my professional as to my personal life. Once war is here, the churches will be called upon to enlist, as will every other social institution. Therefore would I make it plain that, so long as I am your minister, the Church of the Messiah will answer no military summons. Other pulpits may preach recruiting sermons; mine will not. Other parish houses may be turned into drill halls and rifle ranges; ours will not. Other clergymen may pray to God for victory for our arms; I will not. In this church, if nowhere else in all America, the Germans will still be included in the family of God's children. No word of hatred shall be spoken against them—no evil fate shall be desired upon them. . . . So long as I am priest, this altar shall be consecrated to human brotherhood, and before it shall be offered worship only to that one God and Father of us all, 'Who hath made of one blood all nations of men for to dwell together on the face of the earth.' "

A special meeting of our Board of Trustees was called for the next day, Monday, in the afternoon, to consider these things. . . . The Trustees of my church were an extraordinary group of men keenly aware of responsibility in a time like this. . . . Most of them were Unitarians, and thus familiar with the concept of freedom in the religious world. These men . . . were composite in character, but with definite trends, which were bound to assert themselves in all matters of decision. They had agreed to have a private meeting on this occasion, so there was nothing for me to do but sit it out with the reporters, and hope for the best.

The session was not long. It was soon discovered that only one man, in all that group comprising the governing body of the church, was sympathetic with my ideas of war and peace. Almost unanimously, in other words, the Trustees were opposed to their minister in this supreme crisis of the nation's life. But what about the minister's right to preach his gospel to a congregation, and a general public, overwhelmingly in favor of the President's policy of "war to end war"? Could a church be expected to hold together under circumstances of this kind? Was there not a stern and solemn obligation laid upon the citizenry of a country to support that country until peace came again? Failing this, must there not be found some way of dissolving a relationship which must be increasingly difficult?

It was my happy lot, and to the everlasting credit of the Trustees, that in this crucial hour of decision but one issue was recognized as important and relevant—namely, freedom.

After an astonishingly short session, there emerged a single Trustee, who seemed to be charged with the task of announcing, in an informal sort of way, what had been done. Evidently, no formal vote had been put and carried, no resolution had been carefully phrased and passed, no release authorized for public use. The Trustees had taken only a few minutes to define the issue and find themselves all in accord.

"I have little to say," began this spokesman of the Board, "except to emphasize that what we have done was done by unanimous action. We all agreed that the question before us was a simple question of freedom. That to this there could be only a single answer.

"For nearly a hundred years (1825–1917) this church has been a free church. What Mr. Holmes said yesterday was his business and not ours. The Trustees of this church, both as individuals and as officers, repudiate these ideas. This is our freedom as members of this congregation. But of Mr. Holmes's right to say what he did, there can be no question. This is his right as minister of this congregation. So we see no need, or indeed excuse, for taking action in this case. Mr. Holmes will remain here as the minister of a free pulpit in war as in peace, and will pray with us that the grace of God may abide with us, and therewith help us upon our way."

I have had many experiences in my life of more than half a century in the ministry, but I seek in vain for an episode to match this action of my Trustees in the hour of trial. . . . They rose up like men, and struck a blow for freedom. To them be honor and acclaim.

I Speak for Myself, 1958

THE OUTLAWRY OF WAR

The Outlawry of War was the outstanding peace movement of its time [1918–28]. It dominated public discussion for a decade, and worked out, alas too late, the one creative proposal for peace which, for its very boldness, attracted and held attention. From the beginning the Outlawry of War movement was strong in leadership. Its terrific drive, on both sides of the Atlantic, emanated from Salmon O. Levinson, a Chicago lawyer not hitherto known to the pacifist forces of the nation, but who, for the few years before his death, led the way where others followed. Of all the public men I have ever known, S. O. L. was personally the most forceful and untiring. To see him at work was like watching the pulsations of a great machine. He conquered men by overwhelming them. For years he stormed the political citadels of Washington, and secured attention if for no better reason than that he demanded it. It was the case of the importunate widow all over again. But he did not fight alone. Great leaders rallied to his cause. Among these were John Dewey, the educator, Senator [William] Borah of Idaho, Charles Clayton Morrison, editor of the *Christian Century* and author of the textbook on *Outlawry*, Raymond Robins, passionate orator and politician. All these men, and others, I knew and worked with, and am able, therefore, to testify to their greatness of mind and spirit. It was not their fault that we did not succeed. The shadow of the last war lay too heavily upon the next war to be lifted, at least in time.

One had only to read the Versailles Treaty (1919) to know that, if rigorously executed, it would serve only as an entrance-way into another world war. Its terms destroyed the German republic, and removed from Europe any hope of peace. As time went on, the situation grew worse, thanks to Allied stupidity and greed and the sheer weakness of all those liberal forces which were promising to build a new world out of the ruins of the old. The League of Nations, so confidently relied upon to provide a counterweight to the disruptive forces everywhere at large, proved a failure. In a fever of zeal and desperate hope, there suddenly appeared a final constructive movement on behalf of peace, which came to be known as the Outlawry of War. In a few years it gathered such momentum that it assembled the Conference of Paris, which in turn published [August 27, 1928] the treaty, signed for the United States by Secretary of State [Frank] Kellogg, outlawing war as an instrument of national policy.

I Speak for Myself, 1958

TRIFLING

I. Special Cable to the New York Times

Paris, September 10, 1917.—American forces attacked the enemy this morning at LaDun, and captured three lines of German trenches on a front of two hundred yards. The enemy had fifty killed, and one hundred and ten wounded or captured. Our loss was trifling.

II. Article in the Scarboro Weekly Item

The sympathy of relatives and friends is being extended to Mrs. William Brown, of 72 South Main Street, on the death in France of her son, Thomas. News came from the War Department last Thursday that he had been killed in an engagement with the enemy at LaDun on September 10.

Thomas Brown was twenty-three years of age, and was the only son of Mrs. Brown, who has been a widow for many years. After graduating from the grammar school, he went to work at Wilkins' Hardware Store in Bangor, hoping to earn money for his college course at Bates, but after a few months he came home to run the farm and take care of his mother, who had never recovered from a severe attack of pneumonia. Thomas's devotion to his mother was familiar to all of our townspeople, and makes his death at this time particularly regrettable. Memorial services will be held at the First Congregational Church as soon as Mrs. Brown is able to attend.

III. *Advertisement in the Scarboro* Weekly Item

Died On Friday, September 25, Mrs. William Brown, in the 53rd year of her age. Funeral services, and memorial services for her late son, Thomas, at the First Congregational Church, on Sunday, at 3 o'clock. All are invited.

Essay in *Unity*, 1930

SATAN WINS
(See Job II)

Now there was a day when the sons of God came to present themselves before the Lord, and Satan came also among them to present himself.

And the Lord said unto Satan, "Whence comest thou?" And Satan answered the Lord, and said, "From going to and fro in the earth, and from walking up and down in it."

And the Lord said unto Satan, "Thou seemest merry." And Satan answered, and said, "Why should I not be merry? The earth is mine, and all the inhabitants thereof."

And the Lord said unto Satan, "The earth is thine? How sayest thou?" And Satan answered, and said, "Yea, Lord, the earth is mine. I have defeated thee. I have persuaded men to do evil, and call it good. I have taught them to steal with pride, to lie with honor, to kill with glory. I have made rapine respectable, and murder heroic. For thy sake, men do my will. In thy name, they worship me."

And the Lord said unto Satan, "How hast thou done this thing?" And Satan answered, and said, "A little thought of my own—a scheme, a droll deceit! The war in heaven that cast me and my angels into hell—I taught this unto men. Behold, I said, here is a game that has been played in heaven. You should know it. I'll teach it you, if you will stake your souls. And men were tempted, and did fall. And now I go to and fro in the earth, and walk up and down in it, and watch men play this game which casts them into hell with me."

And the Lord said unto Satan, "Hast thou considered Christ, my beloved Son, the Prince of Peace?" And Satan answered, smiling, "Yea, Lord, I have considered Christ, thy beloved Son, the Prince of Peace. Men march to war beneath his cross. It is for him they fight and kill."

Essay in *Unity*, 1930

THE UNKNOWN SOLDIER SPEAKS
(A Sermon for Armistice Day)

It was some years ago that I first visited the grave of the Unknown Soldier in Washington. I thought then, as I think now, that I had never seen a location more impressive than that of the tomb of this nameless warrior. I have stood by the grave of the Unknown Soldier in Westminster Abbey—but here was the open sky as contrasted with the stuffy gloom of the English cathedral. I have stood by the grave of the Unknown Soldier under the Arc de Triomphe—but here was the quiet of grass and trees, and careful footsteps, as contrasted with the noise and confusion of the greatest avenue in Paris. There was something about this American grave that was ineffably beautiful. The simple tomb upon the crest of the hill, the silent temple in the background, the gleaming city in the foreground, and all about, the buried dead who had given "their last full measure of devotion" to the nation's service—it was all something to touch the heart. Only the sun was too bright, and the twittering of the birds too loud! I longed to be here in the mystic hours when darkness might lay its balm upon the tired eyes, and all distraction drift quietly away upon the tides of peace. I wondered, as I walked along, if one could come to Arlington Cemetery after nightfall!

I kept wondering about this matter as I made my way back to my hotel. I wondered about it during dinner, as I sat alone and reviewed the happenings of the busy day. I wondered about it as I lounged in the big arm-chair by my window, with a book of poetry in my hands, and looked out for a moment over the city of Washington to the south. There was the Potomac, losing its luster as the darkness of the night slowly descended upon the scene. Quite a distance beyond was the hill, now no longer visible, and on that hill the Unknown Soldier. What did he think about on nights like this? Did his spirit go wandering back to Flanders Field where he had last seen the light of the sun, and felt the sweet contacts of human flesh? Was he glad the nation had sent him, or was he sorry? Did death seem to him a tragedy, or something else? And what about these honors which were his, and yet not his—did they surprise him, or was he used to them by now? Surely, if one could open that grave, one would meet strange thoughts. And see an unknown man! How quiet it is here! It was possible to get into this cemetery after all. The tomb was beautiful by day, but never so beautiful as now, with the darkness, the stars, and all that distant shimmer of the city. There is the dome of the Capitol— a spot of light, like a door opening into the night. And there is the Monument—that shaft of shadow, lifted up as though in protest, against the stars. And here is the grave, and the soldier, and myself—alone!

I was settling myself down to meditation, when I found that I was not alone. There seemed to be a presence with me. At first it was like a shadow, everywhere and yet nowhere. Then it seemed to localize itself to the right here, between me and the marble tomb. Then gradually, like a ship emerging ghost-like from a fog, it seemed to take on form and substance, and become, as it were, a living thing. I saw a man, very vague in outline and unsubstantial in appearance, but still a man. As my eyes became accustomed to the gloom, I was able to see that he was clad in the uniform of a soldier, and wore the low brass helmet of the battle-line. He was standing as though at attention—tall, straight, and very still. He was obviously a white man, yet the shadow of his helmet, under the stars, made his face look like that of a colored man. He told me, later, that he had been born on a farm in the Middle West. His voice, as he talked, had the broad and cultivated accent of Boston. He had enlisted from New York, so he said, and his name, which I could not hear very distinctly, seemed to be a Jewish name. He was a queer blend of persons and places, this Unknown Soldier. All I could be sure of was that he was an American!

"Hello, buddy," he exclaimed, as he emerged now distinctly from the darkness, and sat down upon the tomb, with a peculiar kind of radiance about his person. He seemed to shine, as though from a light within; yet there was no light cast into the darkness, and the night was as heavy as before.

"Are you surprised to see me?" he continued.

"Well, I am just a bit," was my reply. "I came up here because I thought I would like to be alone, and do a little thinking about you, and this war business, and all the rest."

"Yes, I thought so," he said in a voice still far away, and yet very clear. "And I thought perhaps you might like to talk with me, for I know something about this war business." He stopped a moment, and spat upon the ground, as though there were something bitter in his mouth. "At any rate," he exclaimed, "I wanted to talk with you. And here I am!

"You see," he continued, "I don't very often get a chance at a fellow like you. I spend most of my time entertaining presidents, and admirals, and generals, and visiting diplomats and statesmen—the big bugs that sent us to the war, and would send us again if they got the chance, or felt the necessity. You know how it is—big talk about the flag, and the honor of the nation, and the atrocities of the enemy, while all the time it's debts to be collected, or investments to be secured, or colonies to be captured. The army follows the dollar, you know, and the blood of the army is what makes the dollar pay. I've talked with the dead ones over there. It's the same in every country. They didn't want to fight. They were satisfied enough with their jobs, and their families, and a bit of music, and a game out in the open now and then. Why, a lot of those chaps from Russia and those funny eastern places, they didn't know whom they were fighting, or what it was all about. But the foreign secretaries knew; the diplomats and generals could tell you all the whys and wherefores of the conflict. For the governments make the wars, and we poor devils fight them; the kings and the presidents kindle the fire, and we pour our blood on it, to put it out. And here I have to lie inside this stone, when these fellows come around with their wreaths and their speeches and their tall hats, and I have to look at their silly faces, and wonder what's going on behind. The next war—that's what they're thinking about; and how sweet and glorious it is for the other fellow to die for his country! I wouldn't mind so much if they'd come here to make amends, or to ask my pardon. I could understand if they were clad in sack-cloth and had ashes on their heads. But oh, no! They're all decked out in uniforms and black coats, and they stand up straight, and look big and important, just as though they had done something to be proud of. I'd like to take one of those gold-lace generals, or black-cloth statesmen, that never came nearer than a thousand miles to a battlefield, and show him what I've seen, and make him suffer what I've endured. I'd be happy till the Judgment Day if I could see a foreign secretary gassed, or a diplomat blown to bits, so his very name was lost, and his grave was marked 'unknown.' That would let me rest in peace. all right! I'd never rise up again, to haunt you or anybody else. But that time will never come. The big men play safe, and it's us poor devils as has to pay the price."

"You remind me," I said, as the Unknown Soldier paused for a moment, "you remind me of a little poem that Mr. Chesterton wrote while the war was on. I never understood why the English government didn't arrest him for treason. Listen!—I think I can remember it:

"The men that worked for England,
They have their graves at home
And bees and birds of England
About the cross can roam.

"But they that fought for England,
Following a fallen star,
Alas, alas for England,
They have their graves afar.

"And they that rule in England,
In stately conclave met,
Alas, alas for England,
They have their graves afar.

"That's the idea," cried the Soldier, as I finished the poem on that last, most savage line in contemporary English verse. "I'm not much on poetry—I usually can't understand what it's all about. But that's plain enough—and it's true." And he began reciting to himself—

"And they that rule in England . . .
They have no graves as yet."

There was silence between us for a moment, and then I said—

"It sounds to me as though you didn't want to go to this war very much. Didn't you want to make the world safe for democracy? When your children came to you in after years, and said, 'Daddy, what did you do in the Great War?' didn't you want to be able to look them straight in the eye, and tell them how you fought and bled for your country?"

There was a disgusted snort as I said these words; then there was a long silence. The Unknown Soldier turned away, and looked far off toward the shimmering city, where a thousand lights were gleaming in a thousand homes. As I watched him, the inner radiance of his body seemed to fade, like a dying lamp, and suddenly I felt cold and very lonely.

"Children!" said the Soldier, turning back to me. "It looks as though I should have a lot of children, doesn't it?—Let me tell you how much I wanted to go to this war!

"I came to New York from the West—right off a farm. I had my ups and downs in the big city, but along about 1916 I was doing well. When my father died, we sold the farm, and my mother came East, to keep house for me up in the Bronx. She was a good sport, my mother! She knew I was going to get married, and she loved my girl just as much as I loved her. Never jealous of her a particle! This girl of mine was a teacher up in Yonkers. We had been engaged about two years, and after all that time, we were ready to get married. I'd been saving and she'd be saving, and we had picked out a nice apartment over in Mt. Vernon, and we were planning to set up housekeeping in June, just as soon as the schools were closed. Then in April this war came along. How much do you suppose I cared about democracy, and the war to end war, and the terrible menace of the Germans? That talk was all right for Washington; and it looked great in the newspapers; and it was swallowed like griddle-cakes and maple syrup by those that had nothing else to think about. But it never touched me. I wanted to marry Ruth—and have some of these children they were telling us so much about. Of course, I was selfish, and all that. But I've had a lot of time to think about it up on this hill, wondering what's become of Ruth, just the way she's wondering what's become of me; and I'm inclined to think that loving and having children is just about as important as killing men you never saw and didn't bear any grudge against. Let me tell you how much I wanted to go to this war!

"I wasn't a volunteer, you know. I had to go. This Unknown Soldier here, just like the Unknown Soldier in London, and the one in Paris, he was a conscript. The nation arrested us just as though we were criminals, put us into prisons that were called 'army camps,' and kept us bound until the war was over—or we were dead. It was conscription, that's what it was. That's the only way you can fight a war today—force men to fight it. Don't forget that!"

"But you are forgetting something," I interrupted. "Don't you remember how President Wilson said of the Universal Service Act that it was in no sense 'a conscription of the unwilling'?"

Again there was a scornful laugh. "In no sense a conscription of the unwilling!" cried the Soldier. "Let me tell you how much I wanted to go to this war!

"Do you remember how we had to register, and each man got a number? And do you remember how they had a drawing of numbers in Washington for the first draft, and how the numbers drawn, columns of them, were published in the papers one afternoon? I remember I went to the baseball game that afternoon, up at the Polo Grounds. As I passed through the gate, I bought a paper, as I was a bit ahead of time. There on the front page was the story of the drawing, and the listing of the numbers drawn. I began to hunt for mine—to see if it had been pulled out of the box. I read the numbers in the newspapers until I was dizzy, up and down, up and down, column after column, page after page. Still I read, almost to the end, when suddenly, like a close-up in the movies, I saw my number in figures a foot high. I was one of the men drafted! I looked up in a dazed kind of way and there was the ball game going on, three innings of it, and I hadn't seen or heard a thing. I didn't want to see or hear anything now. My world had changed. I got up, and went home; and I was sick for a week. Then, blamed fool that I was, when the call came from Washington, I answered. Yes, sir, I answered. I didn't have the guts to say no, the way some of the men did. But just like a nice little puppy-dog tied to a string, I went trotting right along. And the flags waved, and the bands played and all the stay-at-homes shouted and screamed, and I said good-bye to Ruth, and I patted myslf on the back for a hero. And here I am—just a dead coward—a man who was too proud not to fight.

"Let me tell you," continued the Unknown Soldier, in a voice that now seemed very near, and terrible. "There's only one sure way to stop war, and that is to refuse to fight. Those conscientious objectors had the right idea. The grave of one of them is worth a million graves of soldiers, known or unknown. I was talking with the English Unknown Soldier the other night—the chap in Westminster Abbey—and he told me about a great Englishman, a member of Parliament, used to be a cabinet minister, what was his name? . . ."

"I think you mean Arthur Ponsonby," I said.

"That's right," came back the Soldier. "Arthur Ponsonby's the man. Well, the Westminster Abbey fellow told me that this man, Ponsonby, had sent a memorial to the Prime Minister, signed by thousands upon thousands of persons who publicly pledged themselves never to take part under any circumstances in any future war. Now, that's the idea! That's what I should have done. That's what we dead ones over here wish to God we had done. But it's too late, too late . . ." And his voice dragged away into silence and the bitter wind. And then I heard, like an echo—"Too late, too late; but not too late now, for the next war!"

"You remind me," I said, softly, "of a book I've just been reading. It's by H. G. Wells."

"Oh yes—Wells," cried the soldier. "I used to read some of his stories—good ones. And I remember reading some of the stuff he wrote about the war, too. Called it a great crusade, and all that."

"Yes," I said. "But Wells knows better now. And he's written this new book to tell us why. It's called *The Open Conspiracy*. He says that the world is in the wrong hands, and that it's going to destruction. He says that right-minded people, the people who believe in peace, and brotherhood, and beauty, must organize themselves deliberately to the end of recapturing the world. They must form an Open Conspiracy, as he puts it, to get possession of power all over the earth, form a world commonwealth, abolish war, socialize the sources of money, and institute an intelligent control of population."

"Quite a program," was the dry comment of the Unknown Soldier.

"Yes," I agreed, "it's quite a program. And the first step is to resist militarism. Let me read you," I continued, "a little paragraph that I jotted down in my note-book only a night or so ago."

I fumbled in my pocket and after some trouble, I found the page on which I had scrawled the lines:

"From the outset," says Mr. Wells, "the Open Conspiracy will set its face against militarism. There is a plain present need for the organization now, before war comes again, of an open and explicit refusal to serve in any war. [This] putting upon record of its members' reservation of themselves from any or all of the military obligations that may be thrust upon the country by military and diplomatic efforts, will be . . . the first considerable overt act of the Open Conspiracy groups."

I tried to read on further, but my memorandum had become dim, and I could not see the words. But I had read enough. I turned to the Soldier, who was very quiet, and thoughtful.

"This 'anticipatory repudiation of military service,' as Wells calls it," I said to him, "is probably what he has in mind when he says that his Open Conspiracy, if it achieves anything, will exact a price in 'toil, suffering, and blood.' He thinks people have got to sacrifice something, if his dream of a better world is ever to come true."

"Sacrifice," said the Unknown Soldier. "I know something about sacrifice. And quite a lot too, about 'toil, suffering, and blood.' And there are a few million other fellows like myself who know the same thing. They haven't all got tombs like this of mine, but they know . . . they know. I should think that Wells could find a few thousand men and women in the world to make some sacrifice for his dream, after the sacrifice we millions were forced to make for just precisely nothing at all.

"Did you ever see pictures of animals back in the old pagan days, all decked out with wreaths and flowers, and surrounded by flute-players and drummers, and led to the altars of the gods, and sacrificed?"

"Yes," I said. "John Keats describes a sacrificial procession of that kind in his 'Ode on a Grecian Urn.' Don't you remember the lines?

"Who are these coming to the sacrifice?
  To what green altar, O mysterious priest,
Lead'st thou that heifer lowing at the skies,
  And all her silken flanks with garlands drest?"

"I don't know anything about the Grecian Urn," said the Unknown Soldier, "but I know they used to take bullocks in the old days, and dress them all up, and play music, and march in procession to the altars in the temples, and then kill the bullocks, and smear their blood all over the place, and call it religion."

There was silence for a moment. I heard nothing but a kind of a sigh, like the moan of many voices far away. Then came the voice of the Soldier, very near now, and very terrible.

"That's what they did to us," he cried. The moan came louder from the sky, like the murmuring of a crowd. "That's what they did to us," he repeated—and the moan became a shout. "They took us like so many animals, and slaughtered us. See, here's the altar!"

As he said these words, the Unknown Soldier stood up and faced his tomb. He seemed bowed down like a man in pain, or very weak. He remained standing there for a long time. Then suddenly he straightened up, and turned back again to me.

"Do you know," he said, "why I cannot rest upon this hill? Why, night after night, I start awake, and look up at the stars? Why I have met you, and talked with you, and said things that perhaps should not be said?"

He paused, as though to catch his breath. It was very quiet now—the moaning of many voices had passed like the wind. The Soldier spoke again.

"There's no rest for me," he said, "no sleep, no peace, because the thing that killed me and my buddies, and that French Soldier and his buddies, and the German fellow and his buddies, that monstrous thing is still alive in the world. It's a religion—the only religion most men know anything about. It's a religion of false gods and blood sacrifice, like the religions of savage tribes. Only it's more cruel, more terrible than these religions, because it demands not animals for its sacrifice, but men—young men, strong men, brave men, the best we have. And this religion that sucks our blood and devours our flesh, we deck in flags, and drench in music, and house in temples, and worship as a sacred thing. There are a hundred thousand altars in America to God and His servant, Christ, but there isn't one of them as holy in the eyes of the nation as this grave of the Unknown Soldier, an altar to Mars, and his servant, Caesar.

"I thought they had gotten through with me," the specter went on, "when they took me out there into the trenches, and blew off my hands, and left me to bleed to death. I thought I had done my duty, when I'd spilled my blood on the ground, and all my veins were empty. I thought I should have quiet and a little rest when they buried me under the trees in the warm French sun. It was lovely out there in that little corner of the grave-yard. But one day they came and dug me up—and put a flag over my coffin—and lined me up with five other chaps whose names were lost, to pick one of us to be the 'Unknown Soldier.' And they picked on me! Then suddenly I was something more than bones and dust. I became a symbol and a name. I was caught up by crowds, and carried along in pageants, and blessed by holy men. They took me back across the seas, and on to Washington. And then we went marching up Pennsylvania Avenue, with fife and drum:

"Skeleton men and boys riding skeleton horses, . . .
Shining in the sun, past the White House,
Past the Treasury Building, Army and Navy Building,
On to the mystic white Capitol Dome . . .
The honorable orators,
Always the honorable orators,
Buttoning the buttons in their prinz alberts,
Pronouncing the syllables, 'sac-ri-fice,'
Juggling those bitter, salt-soaked syllables—
Do they ever gag with hot ashes in their mouths?
Do their tongues ever shrivel with a pain of fire
Across those simple syllables, 'sac-ri-fice'?

"And so they laid me away.

"The boy nobody knows the name of—
The buck private—the Unknown Soldier—
The dough-boy who dug under and died
When they told him to . . .

"And they bring little children to my grave, to teach them
how beautiful it is to be a soldier. And they bring the great
from many lands, with their wreaths and garlands, to show how
wonderful it is for a man to die for his country. And they hold
festivals on holidays, with prayers and songs and magic rites,
to show that here is the altar of the nation's life. Every day they
kill me again. Every hour they lay me fresh upon the altar,
and spill my blood. Will they never be done? Will they never
leave me alone? Am I never to be forgotten, and have my
peace?"

There was a kind of frenzy in the Soldier's voice by now. He
came near to me, and I could see that he was trembling as
though with some great anguish. He threw out his arms to
right and to left, and I saw Christ writhing upon his perpetual
cross.

"Peace," he cried; "where is it? You made me die—and die in
vain. You slew me like a beast upon an altar, then rubbed my
wounds with salt, and stuffed my mouth with ashes. Do you
know what I thought when I went across to France, after I'd
gotten used to the life, and knew that Ruth would remember,
and wait for me? I really thought it was splendid—that this
was the war to end war, a crusade for peace and brotherhood.
It seemed funny to fight for peace, and to kill for brotherhood;
but those that ought to know about such things—presidents,
and Congressmen, and ministers—they told me so, and I believed, and I was glad. And when that grenade exploded in the
trenches, and I saw my hands were gone, and life was going,
I said to myself, 'It's all right, boy. You've done your bit. This
war's the last war. They'll never do this sort of thing again.
You're dead, or as good as dead; but other men, through all the

centuries to come, will live.' And all of a sudden, just as the light was fading out of my eyes, and I seemed to be floating on the tide of a river into silence, I remembered something that I'd learned out of the Bible in Sunday School when I was a boy—something I remember now—'And they shall beat their swords into ploughshares, and their spears into pruning-hooks; nation shall not lift up sword against nation, neither shall they learn war any more. But they shall sit every man under his own vine and fig-tree, and none shall make them afraid.'

"That's what I died for, or thought I died for," said the Soldier. "But look at things now! The same world, the same armies and navies, the same insecurity and fear, the same hatreds and suspicions and preparations for war—and the same super-stition in the hearts of men that it's noble to fight and heroic to kill for one's country. Kill, mind you, not die! We soldiers were drafted by the nation not to die but to kill. The dying was accidental; the killing intentional. That's the whole busi-ness of war—to kill! But whether dying or killing, either way, it's a lie. I know it's a lie, for I've seen God. But you don't believe it—you people who haven't died, and haven't seen God. You won't believe it. And for all the ten millions of us who were shot, and bayonetted, and gassed, and blown to bits, you go right on in the same old way, hallowing war and making it a brave and splendid show. And you even have the indecency to use me and my grave to fool your children, as we were fooled before them, as our fathers were fooled before us, as all men have been fooled from the beginning.

"How long, O Lord, how long, before mankind shall see that war is the blackest lie in hell!"

Again the Soldier threw out his arms in agony, and again I saw the Crucifixion. And through the silence, far away, as though drifting across the seas of time from an eternal past, there came words, familiar words—

" 'My God, my God, why hast Thou forsaken me?' "

A trembling seized me. I tottered as though the words were a rushing wind, and I but a broken reed against it. Instinctively I put my hand upon the tomb to steady me.

"Yes," said the Soldier, watching my gripping fingers on the slab, "It's a good tomb. Nice, smooth stone; simple, in good taste. It's holy, too, like the graves of all soldiers who have had to die, they knew not why. But I know some graves that are holier than this. The graves of men who died because they chose to die, who died without killing anybody, who died not for their country but for humanity."

The Unknown Soldier was very quiet now. His agony had passed. His voice was solemn, as though he were speaking of sacred things.

"There's a grave in Russia, for example, I'd like to see. Just outside of Moscow! The grave of Tolstoi."

"Yes," I said. "There are some words of Tolstoi that I remember: 'I know that my unity with others cannot be shut off by a frontier, or a government decree. I know that all men everywhere are brothers and equals, and that my true welfare is found in my unity with the whole world.'"

"There's a grave in Germany," continued the Soldier, who seemed to stand straighter and taller as he spoke. "It's the grave of Liebknecht, Karl Liebknecht."

"Yes," I said. "They imprisoned him, and tortured him, and killed him, because he opposed the War."

"And in France, there's a grave." The Soldier was standing now at salute very straight and still. "I've seen that grave. It's in the Pantheon. The grave of Jaurès."

"Jaurès," I echoed, reverently. "Assassinated just as the War began for his love of peace."

"And in London, at Golders Green," said the Soldier. And all his body was aglow with light that blinded me with splendor! "There are the ashes of Morel."

"I met him once," I said humbly. "It was after he came out of prison for loving peace too well."

"And in this country," said the Soldier—and now he seemed to flame like the splendor of candles on an altar—"there's a grave here, too, that's holy. The grave of Debs, 'Gene Debs."

There was silence now, as though the host were being lifted in the church. I think both of us were looking at the same picture—an old man standing before the bar of justice, and saying: 'I have been accused of obstructing the war. I admit it. I abhor war. I would oppose it if I stood alone . . . For I believe that nations have been pitted against nations long enough in hate and strife.' "

And now the Soldier spoke again. It was like the voice of St. Michael to the hosts of heaven.

"And there is a grave," he said, "that no man knows. Not in the earth, for it is lost, but in the heart, where it may be found. The grave of him who said: 'Love your enemies, bless them that curse you, do good to them that hate you, and pray for them that despitefully use you, and persecute you; that ye may be the children of your Father who is in heaven, for He maketh His sun to rise on the evil and on the good and sendeth rain on the just and on the unjust.' "

The great words died away, like organ tones. The Unknown Soldier was looming tall and beautiful, like an angel.

"These are the heroes," he said, very gently. "Their graves are the holy ground of earth. Here build your altars of faith and hope and love, and here let the people worship and bow down, and find Great Peace."

The voice of the Soldier was silent. His glowing body began to fade. Suddenly he was a shadow again, and the shadow, a darkness. I was alone. The wind was cold upon me, and I shivered. Then I seemed to start, and wake, as though from sleep. It was the draught from that open window in my room.

I arose to shut it, and my book tumbled noisily to the floor. What was it I had been reading, as I sat down here in this chair, and looked out over the city, and thought of the Unknown Soldier far off there on the hill? Oh, yes—a book of poems! And here was the open page—and two short stanzas. I must have been pondering them, as I fell asleep:

> Who goes there,
> In the night,
> Across the wind-swept plain?
> *We are the ghosts of a valiant war,*
> *A million murdered men.*
>
> Who goes there,
> In the dawn,
> Across the sun-swept plain?
> *We are the hosts of those who swear*
> *It shall not be again.*

Sermon, *The Community Pulpit,*
1928

ARMED FOR THE FIGHT!
(A Story-Sermon for Children)

In years gone by, in a country far away, there ruled a king who had three sons. These sons were born and reared within the royal palace which stood on the summit of a great hill remote from the homes and haunts of men. Down the slopes of the hill there swept the forest, in which the king's sons played and hunted. Around the forest, at the foot of the hill, there ran a lofty wall of stone, on the top of which the king's sons drove their chariots and rode swift horses. Near the palace were gardens with spreading lawns, and leaping fountains, and pools in which to bathe, and the shade of trees where all was cool and quiet in the noon-day heat. And far above the palace there rose ivory towers, tall and beautiful, whence could be seen in the light of dawn or in the falling shadows of the night the countryside to the far range of snowy mountains. Often the three princes, when they were tired of playing in the woods, or bathing in the pools, or loitering beneath the shade trees in the summer noon, would climb these ivory towers and look upon the landscape of their father's kingdom. Here were roads which they had not trod. Here were villages which they had not seen. And far away there to the north was a great city, dark with smoke, which they had never visited. For these princes had always lived behind these walls and always played within these gardens.

Now there came a day when the eldest son prepared to leave his father's palace, for his time had come to depart into the world. And on the morning of that day, the chamberlain of the king came to the prince and said:

"O prince, before thou goest into the world to meet the chances and changes of human fortune, there is one last thing that thou must do. From time immemorial within this palace, the sons of kings have done this thing I say. Deep down within the vaults of this, thy father's house, there is a room, and in that room there stand three altars. Upon each altar there lies a weapon with which a man may arm himself. Now in thy last hour within this place, thou must go with me into this room of arms, and there make choice of the weapon which thou wouldst use in battle against thy fellows."

Having said these words, the chamberlain took the young prince by the hand and led him through the long corridors of the palace. They came to halls which the prince had never seen. They descended stairs far down into dark recesses where no light shone from the outer world. They passed through vaults that dripped as though with water and echoed to no sound but the sound of feet on stony pavements. The torches drooped in heavy air, and the flame of their burning flared and flickered like a dying light upon the walls. At last, suddenly, from out the gloom, there leaped a door, tall, heavy, ribbed with iron, and barred with bolts of steel. On one side of the door there stood a knight in armor black, with shield and spear, and helmet drawn upon his face. On the other side there stood what seemed to be a monk in long black robe, with hands folded upon his breast, and cowled head bent low as though in prayer. Motionless were these two men, as motionless as statues carved in stone, and as silent as a tomb.

The chamberlain approached the door, and paused as though in fear or hesitation. Then suddenly he lifted high his mace, and smote upon the iron ribs—once, twice, thrice. At the third blow, there came a trembling as of an earthquake. The portal groaned and quivered. Then, as though moved by ghostly hands, the bolts and bars flew back. Slowly, silently, the huge door swung, and opened to the gloom of a long chamber which was tall like a cathedral, yet dark and terrible as any crypt beneath its walls.

"Come, my son," said the chamberlain unto the prince now trembling in hand and limb.

Through the door and into the vaulted room they passed. All was still, save for the loud clashing of the door behind them. All was dark, save for the shining of three candles, far away, as at the end of a cathedral aisle. Yet as they burned these candles seemed to shine with ever larger flame, until they shone like stars from out the firmament of night.

"Come, my son," said the chamberlain again. And he led the prince unto the altars, and the candles. And the prince looked, and saw upon one altar to the right, *a sword*, with long, clean blade as white as silver, and hilt that burned with jewels like a flame. And the prince gave a great cry and seized the sword, and lifted it high before the candle's glow, and turned it left and right till all the blade flashed lightnings in the gloom.

"This is my weapon," cried the happy prince. "This shall I use to arm me for the fight."

Then suddenly a blast, as though of death, swept through the vaulted room. Like stars extinguished, the candles disappeared, and all was dark. Only the door swung open to the torches' gleam and showed the way again. Hand in hand along the halls and corridors passed chamberlain and prince. Swift up the stairs they climbed to sunshine and sweet air. Out into the gardens and to the walls they came, and to the gateway of the palace which was to release the prince into the world. Always he clasped the sword unto his breast. But when the gates swung wide, and he gazed upon the roads he had not trod, and the villages he had not seen, and the far shadow of the city he had never visited, the prince gave a great shout of joy. And he lifted the sword, till all the blade was fire in the sun, and he cried again,

"This is my weapon. This shall I use to arm me for the fight."

Then he ran upon the wind, and disappeared. Days passed, and weeks and months, and no man saw him more. But rumors drifted to the palace of war and bloodshed, of fighting men and weeping women, of children wandering in strange places far from home. And now and then there came from far away, like thunder upon dark horizons, the clash of distant arms. And smoke, like clouds of night, rolled upward from the land and swept through the palace and its gardens. And the trees trembled as though in pain, and all the flowers grew pale and drooped them to the ground. Often in these days the two younger princes would climb the ivory towers, to look upon their father's kingdom. And always they would discover burning homes, and wasted fields, and women fleeing like hunted animals, and men stark dead upon the ground. And once they saw the city near the snowy mountains flaming like a volcano in the night.

And on a day a trumpet sounded 'neath the palace walls.

And the gates were opened to a stricken man, gasping and faint upon the road. His face was pale, his eyes fast closed in pain, and all his body bleeding from a fatal wound. But in his hand, firm grasped, there was a sword with blade as white as silver, and hilt that burned with jewels like a flame.

"Quick—or I die," he cried, and stumbling made his way through corridors and halls, down stairs to dark recesses, through vaults that dripped with damp and echoed to no sound but faltering feet. He reached a portal iron-ribbed and barred with bolts of steel. On one side stood a knight in armor black, with shield and spear, and helmet drawn upon his face. And on the other stood a monk in long black robe, with folded hands and bended head.

"Quick—or I die," he cried again. And silently the armored knight moved from his place and smote with his spear upon the door, which swung wide open to the cathedral vault, and to the candles burning in the gloom. Step by slow step the wounded prince crawled to the shining altar at the right, and there with trembling hand laid down his sword.

"I bring thee back," he gasped, with sobbing breath. "Thou hast betrayed me, and my father's rule. And now I die in penance for my sin. To take the sword shall be forever to perish by the sword."

Years passed. And on a day the second son prepared to leave his father's home, for his time had come to go into the world. And to him, as to his older brother, there came the chamberlain, and said:

"O prince, before thou goest from us to meet the chances and changes of human fortune, there is one last thing which thou must do. Deep down within the vaults of this, thy father's house, there is a room with altars three. Upon each altar lies a weapon with which a man may arm himself. Come now with me, and choose what thou wouldst use in battle against thy fellows."

Down through the halls and stairways to the iron door went chamberlain and prince. Still stood the knight in armor, and the monk with folded hands and head bent low upon his breast. Thrice with his mace the king's high officer of state smote loud upon the door, which groaned and quivered and opened as before. There stood the altars, and the candles. And the prince looked, and saw upon the altar to the left, *a piece of gold* bright as a star, warm as a kindled fire. And the young man gave an eager cry and seized the gold and tossed it gaily, like a juggler's ball, before the candle's light.

"This is my weapon," cried the happy prince. "With this I shall buy men, and use them to my wish."

And suddenly there came a chill upon the room, as though snows had fallen and the wintry cold had come. Like fading stars at dawn the candles dimmed and died, and all was dark. Hand fast in hand, along the halls and corridors, passed chamberlain and prince. Swift up the stairs they climbed to sunshine and warm air. Out into the gardens and to the walls they fled, and came at last to the gate which was to open and release the prince into the world. And always he clutched the gold within his hand. But when the gate swung wide, and he saw the roads he had not trod, and the villages he had not seen, and the far shadow of the city he had never visited, the prince leaped and danced for joy. And far before him, like an arrow, he flung his piece of gold, and loudly cried:

"This is my weapon. With this I shall buy men, and use them to my wish."

Then ran the prince and straightway disappeared. And days passed, and weeks and years, and no man saw him more. But rumors drifted to the palace of mighty works—of mines, and railroads, and ships upon the sea. From far away there came the whirr of wheels and the rolling crash of vast machinery. And smoke, like the smoke of battle, rolled from the stacks of mills and factories, and blotted out the sky. And all the landscape withered and turned black, as from a blight. And the far city near the snowy mountains grew like some monstrous growth; and cities everywhere, like cancers, fed upon the soil. And messengers, sent out to spy upon the land and see what horror had sudden come upon it, returned to tell of a great king who ruled in golden splendor, and owned the land, and walked upon the sea, and bought and sold whatever had a price, while men and women and even little children toiled like driven slaves to serve his need. And often in these days, in sore alarm, the youngest prince would climb the ivory towers, to gaze upon his father's realm. And always he would see the gleam of gold and hear the groans of men. And once, as in a dream, he saw the land become a desert, with every grain of sand a piece of gold, and men, like travelers, perishing of famine.

And on a day there came a knock upon the palace gates. Slowly the portals opened, to reveal a miserable old man, with skin like parchment, and hands like claws, and a face like a grinning skull. In his arms were money-bags, and in the arms of slaves who followed him were money-bags, and on the backs of horses and mules innumerable were money-bags.

"Quick—or I die," he cried, and stumbling made his way through corridors and halls, down stairs to dark recesses, through vaults that dripped with damp and echoed to no sound but hurrying feet. Before the iron door, he cried again, "Quick—or I die." And silently the black-robed monk moved from his place and smote with a wooden cross upon the door, which opened wide to the cathedral vault, and to the candles burning in the gloom. Step by slow step, the trembling prince tottered to the altar at the left, and there with bitter curse cast down his bags of gold.

"I bring ye back," he cried. "Ye have betrayed me, and my

father's rule. And now I die in penance for my sin. Alas for the deceitfulness of riches!"

Years passed again. And now the youngest son prepared to do his father's will. To him, as to his brothers, on the fateful day, there came the chamberlain, who led him to the iron door, and to the vaulted chamber, and to the altars and the candles.

And the prince looked, and saw the altar to the right, and the sword with long, thin blade as white as silver, and hilt which burned with jewels like a flame. And he lifted the sword, and held it to his gaze; and lo, from the shining point of the blade there fell, drop after drop, red blood! And the prince, shuddering, put back the sword into its place.

And he looked again, and saw the altar to the left, and the piece of gold, bright as a star, and warm as a kindled fire. And he lifted the gold, and held it to his gaze; and lo, upon his fingers, where they touched the gold, red rust! And the prince, shuddering, put back the piece of gold into its place.

And he looked again, and saw the altar neither to the right, nor to the left, but straight before, and on it *a cup of water.* And the prince lifted the cup, and held it to his gaze; and lo, inscribed thereon were letters which were fashioned into words, and read: "*Whosoever shall give to drink unto one of these little ones a cup of cold water only, he shall in no wise lose his reward.*" And the prince took the cup into his hands, and raised it like a chalice in the sacred mass, and cried:

"This is my weapon. This shall I use to conquer humankind."

Then suddenly a sound like distant music through the vaulted room! The candles glowed like suns, and all the darkness turned to glorious light. With hands firm clasped upon the lifted cup, the prince moved back through corridors and halls, up stairways to the sunshine and sweet air, out to the gardens and the walls, and to the gate that opened on the world. And when the gate swung wide, and the young prince looked upon the roads he had not trod, and the villages he had not seen, and the far shadow of the city he had never visited, he paused, and gazed upon a beggar lying weak and sick beside the gate. And he knelt to the beggar, and gave him to drink from out his cup, and murmuring said,

"This is my weapon. This shall I use to conquer humankind."

Then rose the prince, and went upon his way. Days passed, and months and years, and no one saw him more. But a strange beauty fell upon the land. Man lived at peace with man, for all were friends and none were enemies. At early morn, the people went forth into the fields for happy toil, and in the evening returned to happy play. And they built houses, and inhabited them; they planted vineyards, and ate the fruit of them. They did not build, and another inhabit; they did not plant, and another eat. They did not labor in vain, nor bring forth for calamity; for as the days of a tree were the days of the people. And the wilderness became a fruitful field, and the desert as a garden of roses. And there was no more the voice of weeping, nor the voice of crying. For love reigned within the home and peace upon the mountains. And often, in the eventide, when the labor of the day was done, the king's chamberlain would climb into the ivory towers to gaze upon the land. And to his ears came strains of distant music, and to his eyes the light that never was on land or sea.

And on a day there came great shouts before the palace gates, and the songs of many voices like ocean-waves. And as the gates swung wide upon the world, there entered a man like to an angel, so tall he was, and radiant, and beautiful. And all about him pressed a throng of eager people, wearing various garbs and speaking many tongues. And children, quick with laughter and babbling speech, clutched at his arms and seized upon his robe. And friendly animals were mingling with the crowd— cows with soft eyes, horses with silken coats, patient mules and barking dogs. And birds flew wide above the throng, and soared far upward to the heavens, and sang and sang, as though their little throats would burst. And bright in the sunshine shone a cup, wet with the water of a wayside spring, borne tenderly among the people by a little child who led them.

And the multitude of men and animals swept through the gates, and gathered in the gardens, as though for festival. And flowers looked up to see the light of happy faces, and trees bent down to spread their branches for the singing birds. Alone, from out the crowd, moved the young prince into the palace. Alone he walked through corridors and halls, down stairways and through dark recesses, to a portal iron-ribbed and barred with bolts of steel. And on one side stood a knight who sudden knelt, with shield and spear, upon the ground. And on the other stood a monk, who lifted hands and face as though in prayer. Then, without sound, the portal swung in to the cathedral vault. And all was light from candles blazing like the sun on distant altars; and all was music from the voices of men and women and little children far away.

Straight to the central altar walked the prince, and raised within its light the cup of water. And silence fell upon the place, and darkness like the night. Only one candle burned with steady flame upon the central shrine, and in its light the cup shone bright as gold, and the water red as wine.

"I bring thee back," the young prince whispered in the quiet room.

"Behold thou art the Grail, the Holy Grail, which all men seek, and here may find, and so at last may reach

"That purest heaven; be to other souls
The cup of strength in some great agony;
Enkindle generous ardor; feed pure love;
Beget the smiles that have no cruelty;
Be the sweet presence of a good diffused,
And in diffusion ever more intense, . . .
    So to live is heaven:

To make undying music in the world,
Breathing as beauteous order, that controls
With growing sway the growing life of man."

The Community Pulpit, 1930

"THE PLAY'S THE THING . . ."

My play, *If This Be Treason,* . . . was produced by the Theatre Guild, at the Music Box Theatre, as the opening feature of the season of 1935–1936. The play ran for six weeks, forty-eight evening and matinee performances. It divided the critics, who liked it or didn't like it at all. Stark Young gave it a whole page review in the *New Republic.* It was acclaimed by those who agreed with its thesis, and quite generally neglected by the theatergoing public. So in due course it was withdrawn for lack of support.

If This Be Treason had as its theme the problem of peace in our time; it has been to me an innocent source of pride that my play anticipated, point by point, the Japanese attack upon Pearl Harbor. In my first act I had the bombing of the famous naval base, unprepared and unwarned, the initial action of the drama. The parallelism was exact, save only that I had the surprise attack fall upon Manila rather than Hawaii. From then on, the change was complete as I imagined a pacifist President in office during the international crisis, and before the play was done, I had my President of the United States go personally to Japan, just as President-elect Eisenhower went to Korea [in 1952–53], to explore the possibilities of peace before resorting to the "dread arbitrament of war."

I Speak for Myself, 1958

IF THIS BE TREASON

Speaking Characters

JOHN GORDON, *President of the United States.*
DOROTHY GORDON, *wife of the President.*
ROBERT GORDON, *his son.*
DUNCAN, *Secretary to the President.*
TURNER, *his Press Secretary.*
MISS FOLWELL, *his Personal Secretary.*
DICKINSON, *Secretary of State.*
FULTON, *Secretary of War.*
ALDRICH, *Secretary of the Navy.*
ADMIRAL JAMES.
BRIGHT, *Senator from Massachusetts.*
HILL, *Senator from California.*
WILMOT, *Representative from Illinois.*
FITZGERALD, *Representative from Wyoming.*
SMITH, *Representative from Georgia.*
BRAINARD, *ex-President of the United States.*
LORD CARRINGTON, *British Ambassador to Japan.*
PRINCE YATO, *Premier of Japan.*
GENERAL NOGATU, *Japan's Minister of War.*
BARON ISHIWARA, *Conference Delegate.*
DR. FUJIMOTO, *Conference Delegate.*
TODU, *Premier Yato's Secretary-Aide.*
KOYÉ, *Leader of the People.*
MRS. BANE, *a Washington Dowager.*
MANSFIELD, *a Young Diplomat.*
M. GIRADAUT, *French Ambassador in Washington.*
BRITISH AMBASSADOR *in Washington.*

Silent Characters

ITALIAN AMBASSADOR *in Washington*
MRS. WILMOT
MISS WILMOT

MRS. DICKINSON

MRS. HILL

MRS. SMITH

BRITISH AMBASSADOR'S WIFE

FRENCH AMBASSADOR'S WIFE

FIRST GENERAL

FIRST GENERAL'S WIFE

SECOND GENERAL

SECOND GENERAL'S WIFE

FIRST NAVAL OFFICER

FIRST NAVAL OFFICER'S WIFE

SECOND NAVAL OFFICER

OLD LADY

MESSENGER *from U. S. War Department*

JAPANESE SECRETARY (*girl*)

JAPANESE SECRETARY (*man*)

GUESTS, *men and women, young and old, at the Inaugural Reception. Also servants and lackeys.*

SECRETARIES and SOLDIERS *at the Japanese conference room in Tokyo. Also crowd, with leaders.*

[As Act One opens, the stage setting is the White House suite of Duncan, the President's Secretary, where he and Turner, the Press Secretary, dress for the Inaugural Reception. They talk of the possibility of war between Japan and the United States, contrasting the pacific tone of President Gordon's inaugural address with the bellicose words of his predecessor, ex-President Brainard, in an ultimatum to Japan as one of his last official acts forty-eight hours earlier; Brainard had reacted strongly to the attack of Japanese mobs on the American Embassy in Tokyo and an assassin's attempt on the life of the U. S. Ambassador.

In Scene II, President and Mrs. Gordon discuss with Duncan the intention of Congress to convene the next day and declare war against Japan; Gordon refuses to support such a declaration of war.

In Scene III, the conversation among the reception guests—government officials, diplomats, the President's Cabinet and staff—centers for a while on the famous Koyé, Japanese pacifist and labor leader, and his wide influence among the people of Japan, then veers to news of the President's cancellation of steel contracts that very day because, says Gordon to a Midwest Congressman, they were "part of the scheme to force the country into war." Suddenly Secretary of War Fulton gives the President a cable from Shanghai disclosing the news that Manila has just been captured by the Japanese.

In Scene IV, in the President's Office in the White House, Gordon and Fulton confer with Secretary of the Navy Aldrich and hear details about the destruction of Navy vessels and the loss of sailors and marines in Manila. Both Fulton and Aldrich ask for Presidential orders to mobilize the Army and Navy for immediate action; but Gordon, as Commander in Chief, issues instead commands to the Secretary of the Navy to have all ships on the West Coast return to San Francisco harbor within twenty-four hours and all vessels in Japanese and Chinese waters return to Honolulu; to the Secretary of the Army, to order all army units returned to their posts and all orders for mobilization of reserve officers canceled; and to Secretary of State Dickinson, to send a note of protest and regrets to Tokyo, coupled with a request for the immediate withdrawal of all Japanese forces from Manila, "in the interest of peace and good-will." Convinced that Gordon is either insane or a coward—or both—Aldrich resigns as Secretary of the Navy. As Act One closes, Dorothy Gordon encourages her husband to stand fast.

In Act Two, Gordon, without sleep through the night and assailed from all sides, counsels with his Secretary of State, Dickinson, and is warned by him that these actions may be courageous but they are also foolish. He receives the resignation of his Secretary of the Army, Fulton, and is then briefed by Admiral James on the preparations ex-President Brainard had made in the Pacific for eventual action by both Army and Navy against the Japanese in the expected war. He also hears that Koyé, leading a peace demonstration in Tokyo, has been arrested and imprisoned, and that the Japanese War Ministry is breaking up the peace movement in Japan. When Gordon meets with the committee of Congressmen who are intent on changing his mind and securing his support, he reaffirms his orders of the previous evening to the Navy, the Army, and the Department of State, and refuses to support a Congressional declaration of war against Japan. He summons ex-President Brainard to the meeting and, in his presence, exposes the war plans of previous months and emphasizes his intentions to seek peace, not wage war. The Congressmen accuse President Gordon of treason and threaten him with impeachment. Gordon defies them and announces he will personally carry on peace negotiations with the Japanese.

The Representative from Wyoming says, "There isn't time for impeachment. I demand the President's resignation." As the curtain falls on Act Two, Gordon responds, "Refused. I shan't resign. I can't. I'm too busy. I'm going to Japan, and I'm sailing tonight."]

Act Three, Scene I

[*Tokyo. An anteroom outside* PRESIDENT GORDON'S *suite in the hotel. Two weeks after Act II. Late afternoon.* TURNER *is seated on sofa; in front of him a small table with bottles and glasses.* DUNCAN *is standing at window, left.* MISS FOLWELL *is pacing restlessly up and down.* TODU *enters through door at rear, walks to water cooler on table at right, pours and drinks a glass of water, turns and exits.*]

TURNER. God! These Japs! Are we never going to get any news from in there?

FOLWELL. [*Looking at the door of the conference room.*] No news is good news.

TURNER. I suppose when Lindbergh flew the Atlantic, no news was good news. When President Gordon is in there [*pointing to the door*] begging for a chance to meet with the Premier of Japan, no news is good news.

FOLWELL. It's got to be good news.

TURNER. You mean you think that Lord Carrington [the British ambassador to Japan] is going to be able to persuade those Japanese nabobs that Prince Yato must receive the President? You're crazy!

DUNCAN. They must be *listening* to him! They've been in there two hours.

TURNER. Oh! This international world series! The President makes a grandstand play by coming to Japan. Score one for America! The Japanese Premier refuses to see him, and politely offers a flag of truce and safe-conduct home. Score one for Japan! The British Ambassador intervenes, insists on a conference, and if he succeeds, it will be score two for America. And here I sit! Dr. Fujimoto arrives at five. No news! At five-twenty that Jap with the poker face comes out for a drink of water. No news! At five-thirty Baron Ishiwara leaves. No news! At six-ten, out comes poker-face again, for more water. All water—no news! If a preliminary discussion takes as long as this, the main bout will outlast the war. [*A pause.*] Stop walking, Folwell. You make me nervous. Sit down and have a hari-kari. [*Offers her a drink.*]

FOLWELL. [*Goes to the door.*] No, thank you!

TURNER. Come away from that door. You can't hear anything. These Japanese automatons whisper—they don't *talk*. [FOL- WELL *joins* DUNCAN *at the window.*] And come away from that window. Somebody will be taking a pot-shot at you.

FOLWELL. [*Indignant.*] You've got pot-shots on the brain. You were sure somebody was going to fire at the President on his way from Yokohama yesterday. But no one did. If you're losing your nerve, Turner, you'd better go back to your room, and hide your head in a pillow.

TURNER. I'm not losing my nerve, old girl. I just don't like kidding myself. Don't forget that America has declared war! You're at *war* with that crowd out there.

FOLWELL. Funny! I don't feel even mad at them. And they don't look very belligerent. They seem quite busy discussing things.

DUNCAN. It looks like Columbus Circle on election night. [*Sound of drums and tramp of passing soldiers.*]

TURNER. Well, I guess that sounds belligerent. More troops passing.

FOLWELL. But no cheering, you note! [*Sudden cheers.*]

TURNER. No cheering, eh? The goose-step gets them every time! [*Enter* TODU, *who goes to water cooler, take a drink, and starts to exit.*]

TURNER. [*Sings.*] Water Boy!!!

DUNCAN. [*Stopping him.*] Mr. Todu, if you don't mind. Has General Nogatu agreed to the conference tomorrow?

TODU. Mr. Duncan, your servant. When the meeting is finished, you will be at liberty to inquire the details of Mr. President Gordon.

DUNCAN. Of course. Thank you.

TODU. Thank you!

DUNCAN. It would help, if you could give us some idea—

TODU. War has been declared, Mr. Duncan. I no longer have ideas. With your honorable permission—[*He bows, and goes inside.*]

TURNER. Same to you, if you'll pardon my Japanese.

FOLWELL. Well, what do you make of that?

DUNCAN [*a bit quizzically*]. That it might be a good plan to accept Lord Carrington's offer of a guard!

TURNER [*somewhat more than a bit disgusted*]. That it might be a better plan to accept Prince Yato's offer of a flag of truce to take us home!

FOLWELL. Oh, you make me tired.

TURNER. War declared, the Cabinet busted, the Senate ready to impeach the President before you can say "Senator Bright"—

FOLWELL. When do we get the next bulletin from home?

DUNCAN. It will be just like the last one. "Impeachment resolution before Senate tomorrow." How long does it take a senator to make up his mind?

FOLWELL. Longer than a representative. He has to think!

TURNER. The President hasn't got a Chinaman's chance.

FOLWELL. Who says he hasn't. Why don't you keep quiet if you can't talk sense?

TURNER. What's the matter, Folwell? *You* losing your nerve? Well, I don't wonder—caught here like rats in a trap! This is the biggest fool's errand since the Ford Peace Ship. Five idealists, pretending that one man, all alone, can talk Japan out of war.

FOLWELL. He's not alone. There are hundreds of that crowd who are with him. You heard them cheering him yesterday.

TURNER. And cheering the army today!

DUNCAN. *Koyé*'s followers weren't cheering the army.

TURNER. Koyé's in jail—and most of his followers, too.

DUNCAN. Oh, you think so! Come here a minute, if you're not afraid of pot-shots. See those policemen breaking up that group!

TURNER. [*Going to the window.*] Sure.

DUNCAN. If you will watch the way that group disperses, you will see that they merely move into a wider circle, and then gradually reassemble in another place.

TURNER. All Japs look alike to me.

DUNCAN. Watch them carefully, now. That group over there!

See?—That's trained resistance to the police, like strikers on a picket-line.

TURNER. You call this a strike?

DUNCAN. [*Paying no attention.*] Folwell, did you notice anything peculiar about those troops that scared Turner just now?

FOLWELL. I can't say that I did.

DUNCAN. Well, I did. The inside files of the whole company were unarmed.

TURNER. Oh, come now! You don't think they're running out of munitions.

DUNCAN. *Those soldiers were under arrest!*

TURNER. [*Impressed, in spite of himself.*] You're not trying to sell me a tale of mutiny, Duncan?

DUNCAN. Why not? Perhaps that's the news you're looking for! [*A knock on door at right. They all turn, in surprise.*]

DUNCAN. Come in!

[*There is no answer.* DUNCAN *crosses to the door, and opens it. A Japanese* BELL-GIRL, *in hotel uniform, enters with a folded newspaper in her hand. She is all smiles and curtsies. Speaks in very broken English.*]

BELL-GIRL. If—you—please— [*Holds out the newspaper.*]

DUNCAN. What is this?

BELL-GIRL. If—you—please!— [*Pointing to newspaper.*] This—for—here!

[DUNCAN *takes the paper mechanically. Before he can speak again, the* GIRL *bows, exits, and closes the door.*]

DUNCAN. That's peculiar!

TURNER. Well, a newspaper is a *newspaper!* [*Snatches the paper, and sits down on the sofa. He looks at the paper expectantly, then groans.*] Oh, of course! *In Japanese!* What good is that?

FOLWELL. Read it from top to bottom, instead of from left to right.

DUNCAN. Sure, that's the idea!

TURNER. Wait a minute! Here's some English—*figures! Stock*

reports! [*Starts rattling off quotations.*] "U. S. Steel 70 down to 50; Jennings Steel 130 down to 110; poor old Wilmot—

DUNCAN [*impatiently*]. Quit your kidding, Turner!

TURNER. On my honor—look! [*Holds out the paper. He opens it quickly, and an envelope tumbles out.* DUNCAN *sees it, and picks it up.*]

DUNCAN. What's this?

FOLWELL. Addressed to President Gordon!

[*As they gather in a cluster to see the envelope, the door rear is opened by* TODU. *Enter* NOGATU, *in military uniform, and and* DR. FUJIMOTO *in native robes.*]

DUNCAN. Ah, General Nogatu—Dr. Fujimoto. [*Bows.*]

NOGATU. Mr. Duncan!

[*They bow, and cross stage to door at right, where they pause.*]

NOGATU [*to* FUJIMOTO *in Japanese*]. (That's all right!)

FUJIMOTO. (Tomorrow there will be no difficulty.)

NOGATU. (Not if Yato stands firm.)

[*As they exit,* GORDON *enters. He seems elated, and assured.*]

DUNCAN. Well, Mr. President?

GORDON. [*Rubbing his hands.*] It's all right. The conference has been granted.

FOLWELL. That's splendid, sir.

TURNER. That's great—

GORDON. I meet Yato tomorrow morning at eleven. Dickinson will give you the arrangements.

FOLWELL. We congratulate you, Mr. President.—It's such a relief—

GORDON. And thank Lord Carrington! His intervention tipped the scales. He was magnificent. [*To* DUNCAN.] Have you had any word?

DUNCAN. Nothing, sir.

GORDON [*thoughtfully*]. I see. . . . Well— [*Looks at the three.*] If I am impeached—

FOLWELL. Mr. Gordon!

GORDON. As seems very likely—it will make a great difference. I shall be a mere private citizen, with no authority. [*To* TURNER.] Turner, you'd better go down to wait for the message.

TURNER. Yes, sir! Hopkins is on duty till I return.

GORDON [*to* FOLWELL]. Miss Folwell, I have a special order for you. Go get some rest! You've been at it steadily for two weeks. You need sleep.

FOLWELL. Thank you, but I have too much to do.

GORDON. We can't do anything more now.

FOLWELL. I couldn't rest. Please let me stay.—I must *know*— [*She stops, and seems about to cry.*]

GORDON [*very gently*]. I'll need you to look your very best, tomorrow. I'm counting on it.—Go get some rest.—Executive order!

FOLWELL. [*Resigned, and again composed.*] If I *must*, Mr. President. [*Exits.*]

GORDON [*to* DUNCAN]. You'd better get some rest, too.

DUNCAN. Yes, sir.

GORDON. You're just next door.—I'll knock if I need you.— There's nothing more, now?

DUNCAN. Yes, Mr. President, if you will pardon me. This note! [*Hands envelope to* GORDON, *who opens, and reads from a rough scrap of paper. Looks up, puzzled.*]

GORDON. Where did you get this?

DUNCAN. It dropped out of a newspaper which a bell-girl just brought here.

[*The shouts of the crowd rise outside.*]

GORDON. It's a message—of some kind.

DUNCAN. From whom, sir?

GORDON. [*Turning the paper over.*] I don't know. It's unsigned. Apparently from somebody outside. It reads like a Delphic oracle. [*Reads from the paper.*] "The furrows have been turned, and the seed sown. The brave man trusts in the harvest."

[*Enter* DICKINSON *and* LORD CARRINGTON *through door at rear.* GORDON *glances up.*]

DUNCAN. Oh, Lord Carrington, thank you so much for your help.

CARRINGTON. It was a privilege.

DUNCAN. Thank you, sir. [*To* GORDON.] Is that all for now?

GORDON. That's all, thank you. [DUNCAN *and* TURNER *exit.*] How can I thank you, Lord Carrington. You have saved me from shipwreck at the very start.

CARRINGTON. I was fortunate in having the instructions of my government. When London ordered me to support your request for a conference, in the general interest of mankind—for we're all involved, you know—there was nothing for Japan to do but yield.

GORDON. It didn't seem so, for a while. But your personal appeal, Mr. Ambassador—

CARRINGTON [*quickly*]. And yours, sir!

DICKINSON. I believe Your Excellency enjoys risking your neck for a sporting proposition.

CARRINGTON. Oh, I'm in no danger here. I've been in Tokyo longer than the Emperor.

[DICKINSON *offers* CARRINGTON *a drink.*]

CARRINGTON. Thank you. [*Laughs, starts to go.*] Well, good luck tomorrow! [*Drinks with* DICKINSON. *Then, solemnly.*] And we'll need it! [*Turns to* GORDON.] You've got yourself into a pretty bad hole, Mr. President. For God's sake, see that you get out of it. I must warn you not to be deceived. This was only a skirmish this morning—the real battle comes tomorrow. Prince Yato was what you Americans call "sitting pretty" when he refused to see you. You would have had to return to America, with your mission a complete failure.

Then, unexpectedly, my government forced his hand—also humiliated him before his people. He's had to back down, and that means he's got to regain his prestige. Mr. President, our success this afternoon was too complete. To be frank with you, I suspect a trap—some trick which these Japanese will turn to their own advantage. Look out for a move that may surprise us!

GORDON. I must take my chances on that.

DICKINSON. The President has realized from the beginning that he is facing a gamble.

GORDON. Not so great a gamble as war! In any case, your presence at the conference table, Lord Carrington, will be an invaluable service.

CARRINGTON. But there are limits to what we can do. My government went about as far today as it can go. My presence tomorrow will be hardly more than that of a friendly observer. You must settle things, single-handed, with Yato and Nogatu—and they're dangerous!

DICKINSON. You know, Lord Carrington, I was opposed to this venture. I am here purely out of loyalty to my chief. It was a relief yesterday to see public sentiments so largely on his side. The people seem not unfriendly.

CARRINGTON. Well, of course, there is the phenomenon we diplomats have a way of forgetting. The chemical action of public opinion! There's been a good deal of peace sentiment here for a long time. But don't trust that crowd. It's the government you have to deal with tomorrow. Of course your coming here certainly placed Yato in an uncomfortable position. He's been going along with Nogatu and the militarists. And you come, and demoralize his war-drive!

GORDON. That's what I hoped to do!

CARRINGTON. Yato and his counselors were utterly mystified by what you did. They knew how to deal with battleships, but they didn't know what to do with President Gordon.

DICKINSON. One man—

CARRINGTON [*exultantly*]. The sailing of that single unarmed ship into the war-zone was more costly to them than the loss of a fleet at sea. [*Suddenly stern.*] But now, Mr. President, they propose to have a victory—all the more as we outwitted them in this initial encounter.

GORDON. There is no question of victory, Lord Carrington. I am here to make peace.

CARRINGTON. You are facing an enemy at bay, Mr. President. The sword is out of the sheath. I could almost wish, Gordon, for your own sake, that you had accepted Yato's safe-conduct home, under that flag of truce.

GORDON. [*Aroused again.*] Impossible! You yourself have pointed out the humiliation—and defeat!

CARRINGTON. Yes, yes—forgive me! But you are in danger— physical danger! Let us protect you with a guard.

GORDON. I'm sorry, Lord Carrington.

CARRINGTON. At least Secret Service protection. No one need know.

GORDON. Thank you, Lord Carrington, but I cannot sue for peace with a gun in my hand. I trust my enemy. That is my only strength.

CARRINGTON. Very well— [CARRINGTON *looks at* DICKINSON, *and shakes his head.*]

DICKINSON. You're sure of yourself, Gordon.

GORDON. I must be. [*To* CARRINGTON.] Until tomorrow.

[DICKINSON *hesitates, then holds out his hand. Enter* DUNCAN *hurriedly, carrying a message.*]

GORDON. What is it, Duncan?

DUNCAN. [*Reading.*] The Senate has convened, Mr. President, to take its final *vote on your impeachment.* [*He hands the message to* GORDON.]

Scene II

[*Tokyo. A conference chamber. Noon, the next day.* GORDON, DICKINSON, CARRINGTON *are seated left center.* DUNCAN *and* MISS FOLWELL *left of them.* PRINCE YATO, DR. FUJIMOTO, GENERAL NOGATU, BARON ISHIWARA *are seated right center.* JAPANESE SECRETARIES *sit at a desk down right.* TODU *stands. A loud murmur and shouts from the crowd outside.*]

CARRINGTON. Prince Yato. Gentlemen. The President of the United States has asked me to act as intermediary in this extraordinary session brought about in the interest of peace between your two countries. He wishes me, first of all, to apologize for his unfamiliarity with your language, and to thank you for your willingness to use his. I hope we may have a frank and open discussion of the question at hand: the settlement of disputes between the Japanese Empire and the United States. General Nogatu, Dr. Fujimoto and I have spoken with President Gordon privately, and know his position. I should like him to present it to you. Mr. President. [CARRINGTON *sits down.*]

GORDON. Lord Carrington, Mr. Premier, as President of the United States, I have undertaken an unusual mission in the confidence that I might find, with your help, a common ground on which to settle our grievance without bloodshed. I did this in the full knowledge that it was a new procedure, knowing also that only desperate measures could prevent a more desperate conflict. I count on your discretion.

YATO. [*Pause.*] Mr. President . . . I must reply by being frank with you. We do not know, my colleagues nor I, *why* you have come to our country.

GORDON. Is it unusual, Mr. Premier, for the head of one nation to visit that of another?

YATO. Not at all. I have myself visited your country. But not in a state of war.

GORDON. Because of this state of war I am here.

YATO. For that very reason you should not be here.

GORDON. I have come to end this state of war.

YATO. War can be ended in only one way. By victory and defeat, in battle.

GORDON. Pardon me, Mr. Premier. It can be ended by the agreement of governments, before victory and defeat have stirred up the hatred that makes agreement impossible.

YATO. Your country has already acted—

GORDON. Without my recognition nor sanction.

YATO. That is a matter for you to settle. Your country has declared war without provocation.

DICKINSON [interrupting]. —After your forces attacked Manila!

CARRINGTON. Mr. Dickinson, if you please.

YATO. What motivated that attack? *Your* ultimatum. *Your* fleet maneuvers.

GORDON. I admit that. [Pause.] This is the first point on which we agree.

YATO. You admit a state of war. Why do you refuse to wage it?

GORDON. Because I do not believe in war.

YATO. You do not move your armies nor your fleet. You come here, instead, on a mysterious mission.

GORDON. There is nothing mysterious, Mr. Premier. We are not playing the game of war. That is all.

YATO. I am not sure.

[DR. FUJIMOTO *asks a question, in Japanese.* YATO *repeats* GORDON's *statement. They smile.* ISHIWARA *and* FUJIMOTO *confer. Ad lib. in Japanese.*]

GORDON. How can I make you sure, Prince Yato?—I ask for your confidence.

YATO. You do not *dare* to fight.

GORDON. Mr. Premier, we are not here to discover new grievances, nor suspicions. We are here to prevent a catastrophe! [*Pause.*] I have come to Tokyo at the risk of my office, my reputation, perhaps my life, to stop the war while there is still time.

YATO. You should have thought of that weeks ago, when your President sent the ultimatum to our Emperor.

GORDON. Must we continue to discuss what happened before I assumed office?—I refuse to recognize that ultimatum. I have withdrawn the fleet. I ask you now to risk as much. [YATO *is silent.*] I simply believe that neither of our nations wants war. I have confidence in my own people, as I have in the people of Japan. [*Pause.*] Lord Carrington, will you explain that to the delegates, please?

CARRINGTON. [*Speaks in Japanese.*] (The President does not believe that either nation wants war.)

FUJIMOTO. (America started the war, we cannot help it.)

CARRINGTON. He says America, it's quite evident, started the war, and they can't help it.

YATO. You are here, Mr. President, to take advantage of your high office by watching us, to see what we shall do. You have come to delay our preparations for war. We are ready; you are not! Meanwhile, in America, you *make* ready!

DICKINSON. This is uncalled-for, Mr. Premier! You cannot believe—

YATO. You come to mislead our people, to stir up the enemies of our government. You teach the people that you are their friend, and we are their enemies—and they *protest* against the war. You make us courtesies, and all the time, you stab us in the back.

CARRINGTON. Prince Yato. The President of an enemy nation has crossed the sea, in time of war, at great personal danger to himself, to seek understanding with you. He is the *guest* of Japan—

YATO. Uninvited!

CARRINGTON. Nevertheless, President Gordon is here, in your hands.

YATO. Yes. He is in our hands. And he believes, as you do, that my government will not dare to act against him. [*Pause.*] Mr. Ambassador, you are a statesman. You do not imagine that we can let the President come to Japan with his aides, see, and hear—and then go home?—Mr. President, you will not be permitted to confuse my people indefinitely. [*He takes up the document from the table.*] We have here, Mr. Secretary of State, our terms of peace.

DICKINSON. [*Eagerly taking them.*] At last! Something definite!

[DICKINSON *shares the document with* GORDON. *After a pause.*]

GORDON. Terms of peace, Mr. Premier—or terms of surrender?

YATO. I am glad that you understand, Mr. President.

GORDON. [*Taking document from* DICKINSON, *lays it down.*] I am not here to ask terms. Least of all to surrender.

YATO [*angrily*]. It is surrender—or *fight!*

GORDON. I recognize no such alternative.

YATO. [*Pause. Rise.*] Very well, Mr. President.—I believe this conference is at an end.

[*All the Japanese rise.* YATO *turns to his colleagues.*]

CARRINGTON. [*Rises.*] Prince Yato, may I beg you, in the interest of your country, as well as President Gordon's . . . ?

YATO. I should be a traitor to my country, if I did not fight the enemy when I meet him. The President has refused open warfare. He has insisted instead upon meeting us in conference. The terms offered by me he rejects.—My duty is clear.

CARRINGTON. The President comes trusting in your generosity, your good-will, your love of justice . . .

YATO. In war, Mr. Ambassador, there is no generosity, no good-will, no love of justice. There is only power, force. In war we strike, to win! [*Turns abruptly to* NOGATU *and speaks in Japanese.*] (Arrest him.)

NOGATU. Mr. President, in the name of His Sacred Majesty, the Emperor, I order your *arrest,* as prisoner of war. Todu! [TODU *salutes.*] (Get the soldiers.)

[GORDON *rises, steps back.* TODU *exits and calls command to soldiers.*]

DICKINSON. Arrest? Mr. Premier, this is incredible!

YATO. I am sorry to disagree.

DICKINSON. One moment, Mr. Premier.—General Nogatu! [*Pause.*] If you go through with this arrest, you will be signing your own political death warrant. Your government will fall!

YATO. I am not an idealist, Mr. Secretary. Only a servant of my country. What happens to me or my Cabinet does not matter—

[*Soldiers enter.*]

CARRINGTON. [*Goes to* YATO, *as* GORDON *confers with* DUNCAN *and* DICKINSON.] Mr. Premier, I must, of course, send word of this at once to London.

YATO [*defiantly*]. Yes, to London.—To Berlin and Paris. Let them all hear. The day has passed when Japan was to be frightened by the West.—Have you any further business, Mr. Ambassador? [*Long pause.*] If not, I must proceed with mine. [*Turns to* GORDON.] It is with regret, Mr. President—

DICKINSON. Wait a minute! Are you sure that he *is* the President! [DICKINSON *crosses to* YATO.] Are you so sure? President Gordon is on trial at this moment, before his own Congress. This very morning we may hear that he has been convicted of the crime of trying to make peace for his country.

CARRINGTON. Quite true, Mr. Dickinson! [*To* YATO.] If the President is impeached, you will have in your hands not the the head of a great nation, but a private citizen of as much significance to you as some sentry caught off guard.

YATO. As you suggest, gentlemen. In that case, we need not consider the respect due the President of a foreign power. I shall see that our prisoner receives all the attentions usually accorded—a sentry caught off guard!

[*General consternation among the American contingent.*]

CARRINGTON. Be careful that you don't go too far!

YATO. Are you speaking as Ambassador or as an arbitrator, Lord Carrington?

CARRINGTON. As an Englishman. My sovereign would like to see peace among the nations. In his name I protest this act as a high-handed, militaristic threat which will only succeed in involving *all* of us in war.

YATO [*menacingly*]. Mr. Ambassador, you will stop this insulting interference. Otherwise . . . !

CARRINGTON. Do you threaten *me* with arrest? You wouldn't dare.

YATO. Try me and see. [*Pause.* YATO *and* NOGATU *confer.*]

GORDON [*coming forward*]. Thank you, Lord Carrington. You are very kind. [CARRINGTON *pauses, then returns to his chair.*] Mr. Premier . . . I should like to ask you, as one *man* to another, what you hope to gain by detaining me.

YATO. I am Premier of Japan. I cannot step down from my office.

GORDON. Then perhaps you will listen to one who still has that privilege.—What have you to gain?

YATO. What have I to lose?

GORDON. War! The incalculable loss of war! [*He begins to speak now like a man possessed.*] More terrible than earthquake and famine! Prince Yato, you know something about these horrors—your country swept with ruin, your people dead by the thousands! We have helped you when you were thus helpless before the forces of nature—mourned with you for these lives you could not save. But would you not have saved them, if you *could?* Had it been in your power, as it is now with this war, would you not have stayed disaster before you lost everything?

YATO. We shall not lose the war.

GORDON. Wars are always lost. Victor and vanquished alike, lose everything.—Wealth, trade, productive enterprise, security, your progress through half a century—

YATO. And we gain?

GORDON. Nothing! A mile or two of territory, a huge debt, millions of discontented citizens, the contempt of the world, the curse of history. Weigh *these* against the lives of your young men—millions of them—boys who love life . . .

YATO. Who love Japan, and will gladly die for her!

GORDON. At your order! Mr. Premier, by what right do you give that order?

YATO. The right of my great office, as Minister of His Most Sacred Majesty, the Emperor, Guardian of his Person, Protector of his Honor; the proud tradition of the Samurai which binds us in loyalty to our Sovereign. For thirty centuries we have stood watch about his throne, as stars about the sun, and have not failed. His hand, which touches us as it has touched our fathers, ordains us Servants of the Will of Heaven. This is my right!

GORDON [*quietly, to* YATO]. Mr. Premier, I revere your traditions. But you not only serve your Emperor. You administer as well a modern state. Under the laws of your country, as of mine, murder is a crime. Not even you, Mr. Premier, can take so much as a single life with your own hands. Go out upon these crowded streets. Pick out the meanest beggar in all that multitude of people. Kill him as you would vermin—and you will be guilty of a capital offense. [*With rising emphasis.*] Yet by the stroke of a pen, the whisper of a word, you would send a million of your fairest men to death in battle—and call it glory! What is this myth of war that makes wholesale murder beautiful? Under the sanction of what law, on the tables of what religion, is it written that you may kill, not with disgrace but with honor, if only you kill a million, and not one? [*Pause.*] And remember this, to a million of your countrymen dead you must add a million of mine dead. For soldiers die—but before they die, they *kill*.

YATO. Yet you declared this war.

GORDON. [*With tremendous vehemence.*] No! Never! Madmen in my country declared the war, as madmen in your country provoked it, and as madmen in both countries will fight it.— I have come, Mr. Premier, to stop this war.

YATO. It is too late.

GORDON. It is never too late. Not for those people who are praying for peace.

YATO. There is no way . . . [*He is obviously beginning to be troubled by* GORDON's *plea.*]

GORDON. There *is* a way! When we began our disputes, months ago, there were two paths before us. There always are—paths that divide. We took the path of arrogance and force. The other is still open. Mr. Premier, I have come to take that path—the path of reason. As a practical man, Prince Yato, a statesman who would serve the interests of my country, and of yours, I insist that we make peace—today, when we may both be victors, instead of tomorrow when we shall both lie broken and defeated.

[TURNER *enters, hurriedly, and goes to* MISS FOLWELL, *and delivers message. During succeeding speech, she hands it to* DUNCAN, *who passes it to* DICKINSON.]

YATO. You are an eloquent man, Mr. Gordon. Your thoughts are great thoughts. Confucius had them. Buddha founded a religion on them. But I am statesman in authority and must deal with statesmen in authority. This conference, Mr. President, is at an end.

CARRINGTON. Mr. Premier, I must insist—

YATO. I have listened too long. [*Turns to* GORDON, *as* CARRINGTON *is handed dispatch by* DICKINSON.] I am forced to place you, as a prisoner of war, in the hands of General Nogatu.

CARRINGTON. But Mr. Premier . . .

YATO. The conference, Mr. Ambassador, is ended.

CARRINGTON. [*With splendid assurance.*] The conference, Prince Yato, is *not* ended. [*Indicating message.*] The impeachment trial of President Gordon has been suspended in the United States Senate, pending the outcome of peace negotiations with Japan.

GORDON. Suspended sentence! [*Shakes hands with* DUNCAN. *General excitement.* GORDON *and Americans confer.*]

CARRINGTON. Mr. Premier, you know what this means! President Gordon has won his fight at home. Public opinion has forced the Senate to suspend action. The American people are with him. He speaks now not for himself, but for his country.

NOGATU. [*Intervening sharply, as* YATO *hesitates as though in confusion.*] Yes, Mr. Ambassador—for his country! The head of a great nation. As our prisoner . . .

CARRINGTON. [*Aghast.*] Prisoner? Now?

NOGATU. [*As* YATO *starts to interrupt.*] Yes, we will hold him as a hostage for his country.

DICKINSON. You don't propose to hold the President prisoner— in the face of this dispatch?

[DICKINSON *takes dispatch from* CARRINGTON's *hand. As he does so, altercation breaks out between* YATO *and* NOGATU. YATO *is obviously troubled,* NOGATU *excited and violent. They speak together in Japanese, as* GORDON, CARRINGTON *and* DICKINSON *look on in amazement.*]

YATO. [*Speaking in Japanese.*] (We must be careful, General. Lord Carrington is right—this news changes the situation. We must wait—consider . . .)

NOGATU. (No, never! If the situation is changed, it is only to hurry matters. Action is now imperative.)

YATO. (I shall not hurry matters. That would be fatal. Who knows what will happen when this news is known?)

CARRINGTON. [*Who has been listening intently, translates and*

thus explains to GORDON.] Prince Yato is troubled. He is
worried about the people when they hear about this dispatch.

NOGATU. [*Continuing, in Japanese, to* YATO.] (It will be fatal
only to wait. The public must know nothing until Gordon's
arrest has been announced. There is no time to be lost.)

YATO. (Silence, Nogatu. I am in authority here.)

[*As the two men thus contend, now in open anger,* CARRINGTON
turns again and speaks quietly to GORDON.]

CARRINGTON. The Japanese front is breaking, Mr. President.
Your enemies are at war not with you, but with one another.

[NOGATU, *overborne by* YATO, *is silent. He turns away in sullen
anger.*]

YATO. Mr. President, Lord Carrington, it is obvious that a new
factor has entered into this situation . . .

CARRINGTON. I thought you'd realize that, Mr. Premier.

[*He is interrupted by a wild, ecstatic shout from without. The
crowds are in sudden pandemonium. All look toward the
windows.*]

FOLWELL. [*Jumping up.*] The people have heard the news!

DUNCAN. Turner saw to that!

CARRINGTON. [*Turning to* YATO.] Mr. Premier, the people seem
to have heard the news that we have heard. [*Cheers rise and
fall.*] Listen to those cheers. You cannot take this nation into
war.

GORDON. [*Conciliatory, as always.*] There is no war between us,
Prince Yato. Our people, yours and mine, now stand together.

YATO. I cannot agree, Mr. President. A few wild shouts . . .
[*The telephone rings.* YATO *answers it. Speaks in Japanese.*]
(Hello!) [*The shouts become a roar. Cries of* "Koyé."]

TURNER. What's happening over there?

DUNCAN. I can't see. There's some new disturbance in the crowd.

FOLWELL. Look at that mass of people crowding through the
square.

[YATO *leaves the telephone and speaks, in Japanese, to* TODU.]

YATO. (They're storming the jail—shouting for Koyé. Quick! Find out what's happening.)

[*Exit* TODU.]

CARRINGTON. Mr. President, news has come through. The crowd has stormed the jail.

TURNER. What's that they're shouting?

DUNCAN. Sounds like "Koyé."

TURNER. Yes, that's it. Listen to them.

FOLWELL. Mr. President, that crowd is shouting for Koyé!

TURNER. Duncan, do you see what I see? Mr. President, do you see that fellow they're carrying on their shoulders?

DUNCAN. Folwell, come here and look. They're carrying some man!

YATO. Mr. Secretary—that dispatch, if you please! We have not yet been notified! [*To* FUJIMOTO.] (Confirm that.)

CARRINGTON [*at the window*]. They've released Koyé.

TURNER. That must be he they're carrying through the streets.

NOGATU. (Arrest the President.)

YATO. (No, Nogatu, we can't do that.)

NOGATU. (I know my duty.)

YATO. (Silence, or I shall place you under arrest.)

CARRINGTON. Nogatu is defying his chief.

NOGATU. (I'm going to take him to jail.)

YATO. (Don't be a fool.) Mr. President, in this emergency the conference will be adjourned.

NOGATU. No! No! In this emergency, the *army* will take control!

[TODU *enters*.]

TODU. [*Speaking in Japanese.*] (Prince Yato, Koyé is free! They broke the jail!)

YATO. (We know that.)

NOGATU. (What are the troops doing?)

TODU. (The soldiers will not fire on the crowd.)

CARRINGTON. [*With frenzied exultation.*] Mr. President, the soldiers have refused to fire on the crowd. Koyé is free.

DICKINSON. Good God, this is revolution.

CARRINGTON. [At the window.] Koyé is here!

YATO. [In desperate confusion.] Mr. President, this conference must stand adjourned—until tomorrow.

GORDON. Prince Yato, we cannot wait. Your people are demanding peace.

YATO. My people! That rabble!

[A sudden sound of wild cheering, with rush of feet, without. The crowd is loose, and making for the hotel. The tumult draws quickly nearer. There comes a fierce pounding at the doors, which at last break open. A vast crowd of men and women, in native costume, accompanied by soldiers who have thrown down their arms, sweeps into the room. The Japanese counselors are swept aside. At the height of the turmoil enters KOYÉ, a majestic figure, in tattered prison garb, his chest bare. He is very calm. He walks slowly to GORDON.]

KOYÉ. Mr. President. I come to welcome you in the name of my people, and to claim you as a leader.

GORDON. Koyé!

KOYÉ. We were called to fight against your people. We did not want to fight. What quarrel had we? We were happy in our homes, and on our farms. What do we ask—only to be let alone!

GORDON. As people everywhere want to be left alone!

KOYÉ. But what could we do? We were not strong. We were beaten, crushed, we had failed. Then suddenly, Mr. President, as a spark from tinder, the miracle flashed across the sea. You were coming to Japan! In a day, the word had gone to every corner of the land, like the wind rustling the leaves of a forest. No village so remote it did not hear—no man so humble he did not understand. President Gordon coming to Japan to ask for peace! At that moment, Mr. President, as though the heavens had spoken, war became impossible. Your coming was the sound of gongs before our altars. Your presence more terrible than an army with banners. We knew that America wanted peace and would bring us peace. We saw a friendly host reaching out their hands in brotherhood. We were glad, and suddenly we were brave!

NOGATU. [*In Japanese.*] (Treason! Treason!)

KOYÉ. Yes, General, treason if you will. It is nothing new, the call of *liberty is as old as the world.* Listen to it, or are you so old in the ways of war that you are deaf to the people when they call for peace?

NOGATU. (Peace!)

KOYÉ. We played fair, General. We gave you your chance. But the moment you gave the order for my arrest, I knew—the people knew—we were stronger than we had dared to hope. With America we were your masters . . .

NOGATU. (Masters!)

KOYÉ. What a fool you were to make me a martyr to this cause. See! See! [*Holds out his hands and arms, bleeding.*] These scars! *They* have beaten you. My chains have made us free. [NOGATU, *like a furious animal, makes a sudden move—dashes at* KOYÉ. *The two men stand face to face for a moment. Then* NOGATU *backs away, as though dazzled and afraid. Then, forgetting everything, he calls for guards—gives orders, as though in command.* KOYÉ, *with superb serenity and quiet, continues.*] No, General, you have no guards. [NOGATU *looks around as though in amazement.*] What need we of guards? The people now rule themselves—and you. [NOGATU, *with a hoarse and angry cry, rushes to the door.*] You are free to go, Nogatu. But where will you go? Everywhere you will find the people. On the streets, through the city, in the highways and in the villages, to the slopes of Fujiyama—only the people! They will not hurt you—but neither will they heed you! [*Majestically yet pitifully.*] Poor fool, your day is done! [NOGATU *crumples, baffled and beaten. A messenger enters and speaks to* YATO.]

GORDON. You are a brave man, Koyé. I salute you!

KOYÉ. [*Steps to* GORDON.] A common man! But you are President Gordon. Your faith gave me opportunity, your courage brought me strength. Without you, I would be crying to the stars, unheard. [*Firmly.*] Mr. President—you came for peace, and we bring you peace.

GORDON. It is your voice, Koyé, that I have waited all these years to hear.

KOYÉ. And I, yours!

YATO. [*Stepping forward.*] President Gordon, Mr. Koyé . . . [*He bows ceremoniously.*] His Sacred Majesty, the Emperor, asks your presence.

[*Pause, all amazed.* KOYÉ *speaks in sudden triumph.*]

KOYÉ. One second out of all the centuries has called, and we have answered. Worlds have waited for this hour, and we have not failed. The myriad dead in every land, asleep in bloody and silent graves, they have not died in vain!

[*The two men clasp hands and hearts, as by a common impulse. The end has come.* GORDON *seems rapt, to be looking and thinking very far away. A smile of wistful wonder flits across his face, as he speaks words strangely and beautifully familiar.*]

GORDON [*slowly, very quietly, as though reading from some hidden scroll of memory*]. "Not by might, nor by power, but by My spirit, saith the Lord."

CURTAIN
If This Be Treason, 1935

On October 23, 1935, a letter marked "Personal and Confidential" was sent from The White House in Washington. It read:

MY DEAR MR. HOLMES:

    I want to thank you many times for your kindness in giving us the tickets for the play on Monday night. I was very much interested in it and think it was well acted. Some of the characters amused me enormously and I could see them on the Washington stage!

You will forgive me, I know, if I tell you I think it is a valuable contribution, but I think you have made the problem appear too easy. It is not just a question of good will. That is part of it, but not the whole. The causes of war lie rooted in material greed and difficulties of trade and commerce, which are controlled by a few individuals and vast financial concerns and in the growth of populations.

I feel, for instance, that without the agitation and perseverance of the peace groups in this country, Congress would never have passed the neutrality resolution of last year, but the passage of that resolution does not prevent individual congressmen and senators from coming to the President to try to have the particular product of their district kept off any list which is considered "munitions of war."

There is so much to be done before the people are really going to be practical and work systematically toward better international understanding; but I think every play such as yours, every word which is spoken, and every book which is written on the subject is just that much to the good, and I am deeply grateful to you for what you have done.

Very sincerely yours,
ELEANOR ROOSEVELT

IV

THE SOCIAL PROPHET

Fight on, brave spirit, till the evil day
Shall wane; fight ever till the dark, foul blot
That stains our honor be wiped out, forgot,
And right shall conquer, wrong be purged away.
In time to come, it may be, one shall say,
Treading along some long-familiar spot,
"A Parker walked here and we knew it not,
A living flame that dwelt in mortal clay."

The loving hearts that view thee—undismayed,
Full panoplied in all the Spirit's might,
Tongue tipped with holy fire, and unafraid
Of gibes and sneers, gaze fixed upon the light—
Shall bring their marshalled forces to thine aid,
Till Justice conquer, wrong give place to right.
>   —WALTER SWISHER,
>   "A Parker Walked Here," 1910,
>   dedicated to J.H.H.

THE SCANDAL OF DENOMINATIONALISM

The trouble with all these attempts to do away with the blight and scandal of denominationalism is the same; and this trouble is one which carries us straight to the portals of what I have called the "community church." It introduces us immediately to the problem of that new religion which is to be the spiritual expression of our new democracy. All of these endeavors after church unity are vitiated by the common error of beginning operations with the church. They accept the church as a holy thing, a basic thing; and from this hypothesis of a sanctified institution they move to the problem of society, and strive to adapt this problem to the accepted hypothesis. In other words, they are guilty of the fundamental blasphemy of believing that society was made for the church and not the church for society. Nothing can ever be accomplished in the direction of achieving that one religion which must be the expression of the highest and best in the one great soul of man, until we begin our work with men. We must plant our feet upon the earth, plunge into the flowing stream of human life, and here lay hold upon the elements of our problem. Men and women, the people, the masses, the multitudes, the great democracy of the common life! This is our material—this is our problem. Let us forget that there are such things as churches. Let us shut out of our minds, if needs be, the whole story of Christian history. Let us take men just as they are today, and as though beginning anew upon the creation of a new world, ask ourselves what can be fashioned which shall give expression and service to the spiritual needs of the race. Democracy, as we know it today, must build afresh its own institutions. Some of these institutions, the school, the state, for example, it has already produced. Out of the soil of its own life have sprung the agencies of its redemptive action. The church, however, as it still exists today, is an alien. It is an importation from abroad; it is in nearly every case something which is imposed from above. Our talk, therefore, is the reverse of everything we have attempted before. To move not from the church to society, but from society to the church—this is our line of progress! The new tabernacle of God, the revelation of St. John to the hands of angels, is to grow up out of the earth as from the souls of men. This is "the community church" to which I am leading your thought. This is the institution which shall embody the new religion of the new democracy, which shall know no denominationalism, but on the contrary, shall be as wide as humanity, human dreams! Do you remember the little poem which tells the story of the minister who could not find God? Day after day he mounted high into the steeple of his church and there sought and prayed for the divine Father. At last, as though in answer to his prayer, there came a voice. "Where art thou, God?" cried the earnest man. And there came back to him, you remember, that great reply—"Down here among the people!"

Sermon, "Denominationalism:
Religion Inside the Churches,"
The Messiah Pulpit, 1919

IMPOTENCE OF THE CHURCHES

In nothing is the story of our age more remarkable than in the failure of organized religion to play that important part in the determination of events which marked its activity during the Middle Ages, and in the later more stirring period of the Reformation. How can this fact be explained save on the theory that the churches are not interested in those things which most concern the life of the modern man? . . . [These things] are the conditions of his daily life and labor, his conquest of the ills which sap his strength and blast his happiness, his struggles against injustices that deny him liberty, exploit his toil and rob his children of their heritage. They are the dreams and passions of his soul, writ large for our instruction in the great movements of social betterment which have swept the world like cleansing floods in the last one hundred years. The suppression of the slave trade, the abolition of chattel servitude in America, the extension of the franchise, the advancement of education, the emancipation of women and of labor, the care and protection of children, disarmament and international peace, social justice as applied to wages, hours, employment, housing, health, public ownership of natural resources and democratic control of industry—these are the things which have held his heart, and prompted glad hazard even of life on their behalf. These, and not the Fall, the Incarnation and the Atonement, constitute the drama of human destiny, as we understand it at this moment; and it is in the cast of this drama, that the churches, both Protestant and Catholic, do not appear at all. . . . The churches have been either indifferent or ineffective, or—as in the anti-slavery movement yesterday and the labor movement today—utterly and shamelessly antagonistic.

. . . Say what we will, hope what we may, the churches that stand in rural lanes and in city avenues are not interested in the social passions of the hour. They do not function in those fields of life which are today being watered by the tears and blood of men. They are of no effect in politics; they are silent on the woes of women; they are nationalistic sycophants in the vast issues of war and peace; even in the traditional activities of charity and social welfare, they are all but ousted from the field by special agencies created to do work which the churches should never have allowed to pass from their control. All about us are the pressing problems of modern life, in their manifold political, economic and industrial phases. These problems are stirring men to the bottom of their souls, prompting them to sacrifices akin to those of the early Christian martyrs, because they know that out of these proceed the issues of life. . . . This, as we see it, is the trouble with the churches. They are interested in what does not concern modern man, and *not* interested in what *does* concern the modern man. Hence the gulf of separation which now divides the churches from the world!

. . . We have no confidence in the churches, either Protestant or Catholic, liberal or orthodox, as they exist and work among us at the present moment. . . . They serve no purposes of vital moment, are directed to no ends of eternal and universal portent.

There was a time when religion was in the churches. It was the time when men and women were willing to die for the altars at which they worshiped, and the creeds in which they believed. Who thinks it worth while, however, to lay down his life for the churches today? Who would go to the gibbet, or the stake, or the cross, stop the mouths of lions, "be stoned, sawn asunder, slain with the sword, wander about in sheepskins and goatskins, . . . in deserts and in mountains, in dens and caves of the earth," for the sake of Presbyterianism, Episcopalianism, Methodism, Universalism, even Protestantism? How change so lightly from one church to another, or abandon churches altogether, if such loyalties really matter? It is not that men have forgotten how to die or to be loyal. The call of country summoned men in the Great War to sacrifices which it is inconceivable they would have made for any church. Which means that religion has disappeared from the churches as water from a reservoir, not because the springs have run dry, but because they flow in other courses!

New Churches for Old, 1922

AN ANTIQUATED ATMOSPHERE

From the lives of the majority of our people, the churches have disappeared. Those who today support and attend them are members of a generation reared to the practice of religious observance. The new generation has broken free, and turned to other things. Once the channel in which flowed the swelling stream of life, the churches are now become stray nooks and corners in which eddies stir. These eddies not infrequently make much noise; they whirl with a foam and fury that attracts and holds attention. But they are turning always upon themselves; are uncaught by the majestic flow of that central current which seeks increasingly the sea; and, in the end, are doomed to become but "a fen of stagnant waters," choked with dead debris. . . .

Just to attend a religious service on Sunday morning is to witness a spectacle which demonstrates in vivid dramatic form the alienation of the modern mind from all that is most real and precious to the church. Here is a building, the architecture of which is a more or less feeble attempt to perpetuate the glories of Medievalism or the rigorous austerities of Puritanism. Here is a literature, offered as sacred, which contains no word written down later than two hundred years after the death of Jesus, and no idea later than the Neo-Platonic speculations of Alexandrian Judaism. Here are readings, prayers, instructions, exhortations, couched in language Pauline, Augustinian, Lutheran, Calvinistic, Wesleyan, and therefore as unintelligible today as the jargon of alchemy or astrology. Here are ideas which embody science, history, psychology, philosophy, of a type which has disappeared long since from every hall of learning, and from all literature save that specifically labeled "religious." Here is an attitude toward the universe, toward life and its destiny, toward society and its problems, which is as strange to the modern man as that of a foreign country, a distant age, or even another planet. Above all, there is an atmosphere in this place which seems as remote from our everyday world as the atmosphere of a buried city; from it there seems to be excluded everything that breathes of life and joy. . . . Compare a religious service, for example, with a political rally, a patriotic mass meeting, or a public gathering on behalf of some great movement for social betterment! Is it not evident that in the latter we have a vital interest, and in the former a dull conformity to tradition?

. . . Shall we follow the churches' own example and take their creeds as the evidence of what they are standing for in this modern age? By what hocus-pocus of interpretation can these platforms of faith be presented as anything other than what they really are—a record of controversies long since forgotten and of beliefs long since disproved? By what imaginable reversion of attention can persons who have learned the lessons of Newton and Darwin, and are now sitting at the feet of Bergson and Einstein, be persuaded to hold interest in affirmations of the Trinity, the Atonement, the Resurrection, Redemption, Salvation, and the rest—much less to express their spiritual ideals in terms of these conceptions? We do not expect men today to light their houses by rush-light, to travel in stage-coaches or on horseback, to converse in Latin, to live in the thought-world of Plato, or Kant, or even Herbert Spencer. Why should we expect them to accept the ideas or even retain the phrases of the Nicene Creed or the Westminster Confession?

. . . What is essential in the churches is their service of righteousness, their steadfast witness to moral precepts and spiritual ideals. In an age surrendered to the grossest forms of materialism, the churches [must] keep alive the thought of God and the vision of His holy spirit. In a period which seems to have lost all sense of moral values, the churches [must] impose standards which shall some day be the salvation of the race. At a moment when society seems to be given over utterly to hatred and bitterness, to strife, contention and barbaric slaughter, the churches [must] proclaim unfalteringly the truth that love is the sole and perfect law of life.

New Churches for Old, 1922

THE REVOLUTIONARY FUNCTION
OF THE MODERN CHURCH

The church will care not so much for rites of baptism as for public baths and playgrounds; not so much for the service of Communion at the altar, as for that wider communion at every hearthstone which shall give bread to all who hunger and drink to all who thirst; not so much for clerical robes and choir vestments, as for clothing for all who are naked; not so much for splendid churches and towering cathedrals, as for decent and comfortable homes for all men, women and children; not so much for an atmosphere of prayer and worship in the church edifice, as for fresh air to breathe in the tenements and slums; not so much for teaching men to believe, as for giving them means wherewith to live; not so much for keeping Sunday inviolate from open theaters and concert-halls and sports, as for keeping every day inviolate from dishonest stock-transactions, piratical business deals, child labor, starvation wages, preventable diseases, selfish wealth and grinding poverty; not so much for saving the heathen overseas, as for saving the Christians who are perishing at our very doors; not so much for emancipating men from what we call sin, as for emancipating them from the conditions of life and labor which make sin inevitable; not so much for saving souls, as for saving the society which molds the soul for eternal good or ill.

The Revolutionary Function of the
Modern Church, 1912

THE REDEMPTION OF SOCIETY

... The church must shift its emphasis from the problem of saving the individual to the problem of saving society. It must focus its attention not upon individual men but upon man in the mass; it must take as its aim not primarily the salvation of the soul but the redemption of the world; it must realize that its highest achievement is not the filling of a monastery with monks and nuns, nor the crowding of a mourners' bench with repentant sinners, not the administering of sacraments nor the converting of the unforgiven—nor even the cultivation of character—but the building of the Kingdom of God upon the earth.

Here is the world with its hungry to be fed, its naked to be clothed, its sick to be healed, its imprisoned to be emancipated. Here is the world with its evils to be extirpated, its misery to be banished, its injustice to be cured, its sorrow to be turned to joy. Here is the world with the strong preying upon the weak, . . . the rich grinding the faces of the poor, the few reveling in the luxury and ease which is builded upon the wretchedness of the many. Here is the world with its international hatreds and racial prejudices, with its rotten politics and corrupt business, with its passion for riches and its lust for power, with its industrial injustice and its social inequality. . . .

The work of the church, I say, is the work of social redemption. In the pursuit of this work, the true church will grapple with the problem of poverty. It will accept the doctrine of the best social authorities of our time that poverty is due not to individual depravity or individual inefficiency, but to social maladjustment, and upon the basis of this doctrine will so readjust social conditions that poverty will be as impossible as wealth. In pursuit of its true work, the church will enter upon the task of reconciling the hostile races of the world. . . .

No longer will the church be regarded simply as an abode of refuge for the sick, the discouraged, and the oppressed. Rather will it come to be regarded as an armory whence the soldiers of God shall march forth to battle against the legions of Satan. No longer will the church be regarded merely as an assemblage of those who have fled from the evils of a lost world, and have sought their personal safety within the sanctuary. Rather shall it come to be regarded as the army of those who have enlisted for a great war, and are willing to die for the cause which they have espoused. No longer will its work be done by priests who merely pray and preach, marry the living and bury the dead— rather shall this work come to be done by a new priesthood, which shall include not merely the minister, but the merchant also and the politician, the physician and the sociologist. . . .

Sermon, "The New Work of the
Church," *The Messiah Pulpit*, 1909

THE NEW ENSLAVEMENT OF THE NEGRO

The condition of the Negro in the South today is an unspeakable disgrace to that American civilization of ours which we are fond of describing as founded upon the basic principle that "all men are created free and equal"; and it is destined to be, I believe, centuries hence, one of the wonders of human history that in the face of the oppression which is being visited upon ten millions and more of our fellow-citizens at this moment, the rest of us are contented to remain silent and indifferent.

The political freedom of the black man in this country was purchased at a price which staggered the world. Blood poured forth like water, treasure was expended at the rate of millions a day, not in order that the Union might be preserved, but, more, that the Negro might be emancipated from the bonds of chattel slavery, and a government of the people, for the people, and by the people might for the first time be established upon the earth.

A full half-century has passed away since that momentous struggle was completed, and yet today, when we turn to the South and ask regarding the condition of our black brother, for whose freedom *our* fathers paid so dearly, we find that his condition is little better than that of *his* father, who was bought and sold upon the block. "The Negro today," says an influential New York clergyman, "is free on paper, the black man is one of our fellow-citizens in theory. He is reckoned as a man and not as an animal on the tables of the United States census." But, as a matter of fact, in the everyday world of practical affairs the Negro is still a slave, and if there is anything that is perfectly plain in the public sentiment of the South, it is that the Negro shall be made to keep that place of shameful subjection from which we believe he had been rescued by the blood and fury of the great rebellion. He is denied the ballot. He is socially ostracized. He is excluded from public buildings, railroad stations, libraries and theaters. He is denied justice in our courts. He is held as a peon on countless plantations. He is oppressed, degraded, enslaved in every political, industrial and social relation.

And yet, in the face of this unspeakable situation, we find the people of the North indifferent and complacent, and whenever any brave man arises to speak his condemnation of this inequity, he is denounced as a careless agitator and ignorant fanatic. On every hand we are being told that the Negro question is too delicate for public discussion, and that we must leave this problem to be worked out naturally and quietly by the passage of time. We are told that to discuss this question upon a basis of simple justice would hurt business—as though business were of any importance when the life, liberty, and happiness of millions of human beings are at stake. We are told that to discuss this question would offend the Southern whites—as though it were not our duty to offend them when they are the arrogant and blinded oppressors of an entire people. Are they not offending us, I should like to know, by their denial to the black man of those rights to industrial opportunity and political independence which had been bought and paid for by the blood of tens of thousands of heroic men? We are told that to discuss this question at the present time is inexpedient—as though expediency should ever be consulted when "wrong rules the land and waiting justice sleeps." The truth of the matter is that there is but one thing to be considered here, and that is that ten millions and more of our fellow-citizens are being denied those rights and privileges which are legally and morally theirs, and any man who is silent in the face of this oppression is himself a partner to the crime which is being committed. Business, the feelings of our Southern fellow-citizens, questions of expediency—all these things must be cast aside once and for all, and like the Hebrew prophets of old, we must lift up our voices and spare not! It is with the Negro question as with every other great social question of our time. . . .

We are face to face here, after all, with a second great struggle for the emancipation of an enslaved people; and in this second struggle we must take as our motto the words which were made immortal by the great abolitionist [William Lloyd Garrison] who was the leader of the first great fight for liberty here in America: "I am in earnest, I will not equivocate, I will not excuse, I will not retreat a single inch, I will be heard." If this is to be the spirit of the National Association for the Advancement of Colored People, as I believe that it is, its work is the work of God, and even though its numbers may at first be few, it may content and strengthen itself with the thought that its two or three on the side of God are the majority.

The new enslavement of the Negro manifests itself in strange and various forms, but perhaps the most cruel and inexcusable of them all is that which we know as disfranchisement. . . . The Negro in the South today is disfranchised almost as effectively as before the Civil War, and disfranchised not because of illiteracy, but because of color. . . . The one thing for which our country stands, as we like to think, is free government, and the very essence of that freedom in government is the exercise by all men of the right of franchise. The ballot is the instrument of democracy, and the ballot box is its symbol. All the long battles for political freedom have centered around this very question of voting. . . .

It is to my mind the crowning iniquity of these laws of disfranchisement . . . that they . . . make a mockery of the religion of human brotherhood which we profess to practice . . . [and] use all the power of the State to make impossible the realization of this supreme religious ideal. For while I believe that the Negro is in no way constitutionally inferior to the white—while I believe that he is capable of endless development in all civilized practices and achievements—while I believe that the door is open to him into all the realms of music, arts, poetry, religion, I also believe that the erection of a foolish prejudice into a basis of government and a condition of social organization, which is the immediate result of disfranchisement laws, is bound to degrade the Negro, to reduce him to a level of inferiority where he does not naturally belong, and thus shut him out forever from the circle of the human family. You may educate the Negro industrially for a thousand years—you may teach him to grow the best sweet potatoes in the Western Hemisphere—you may make him supremely efficient as a "hewer of wood and drawer of water," but if you refuse to him the equal rights to citizenship, you perpetuate and sanctify prejudice, and thus postpone indefinitely all hope of that human brotherhood of which every true prophet has dreamed, and for which every true servant of humanity has bravely labored. . . .

Address, "The Disfranchisement of the Negro," at the Second Annual Conference of the National Association for the Advancement of Colored People, 1910

THE POLITICAL FUTURE OF THE NEGRO

In this country, as in England, the foundations of social life are shifting. Our democracy, for long political in character, is now becoming fundamentally economic. This means temporarily the predominance of capital; it means ultimately the triumph by the working man and the working woman. The Negroes are pre-eminently workers. Ten millions of them fill the ranks of labor, and therewith sustain the structure of the world. More and more with every passing day is this labor place and power destined to count in terms of social influence. It is in this new commonwealth of toilers that the Negroes, with all other workers, are to find liberty at last. Cling therefore to your place; dignify it, ennoble it, glorify it; it is the seal of your power and the sign of your deliverance. A new world is on the way—and in this world the beads of honest sweat upon the brow of black and white will be the sole crown of sovereignty. . . .

Do you not realize to what an extent we hold the balance of power in legislative and Congressional districts, and even in the Presidential campaign itself? Do you not realize to what an extent the organized exercise of this balance of power can bring us anything that we really want? . . .

We have shown what can be done by non-partisan political

action as applied to our own especial needs and hopes. Following the fight on the Dyer Anti-Lynching Bill in the last Congress, we defeated, by a solidly massed colored vote, four enemies of the Bill—in Delaware, in the 9th Congressional District of New Jersey, in the 6th Congressional District of Michigan, and in the 5th Congressional District of Wisconsin, the sitting Representative was in each case defeated on this one issue, by the Negro vote alone. Keep it up—till every Democratic and Republican politician in the land trembles to his shoe-tops when he looks a black man in the face. . . .

It is in this final emancipation of the commonwealth of workers that I find the real promise of your political future. Not what a man comes from, but what he is—not the blood in a man's veins, but the work in his hands—not the color of a man's skin, but the texture of his spirit—this shall be the stamp of manhood and the badge of citizenship. Here as common toilers on the common way, we stand together side by side. What matters, then, our race? Have we not humanity to brother, and God to father? Are we not one family?

> Come, clear the way, then, clear the way,
> Blind creeds and kings have had their day.
> Break the dead branches from the path,
> Our hope is in the aftermath—
> Our hope is in heroic men,
> Star-lit to build the world again.
> To this event the ages ran:
> Make way for Brotherhood—make way for man.

> Address, "The Political Future of the Negro," at the Fifteenth Annual Conference of the NAACP, published in *Unity*, July 24, 1924

THE NEW PALESTINE OF ZION

There is [in Palestine] the old, non-Zionist Jewish community—those scattered remnants of the old Israel in Jerusalem, Hebron, Safed. . . . [Following] the great invasion and conquest of Titus in the year 70 A.D., . . . Jews were left behind after all the burning and slaying—a miserable remnant, hiding in the mountains, clinging to the ancient shrines, worshiping still their fathers' God. And that remnant has survived the ages! . . . With the unexampled tenacity characteristic of the tribe, these Jews still endure—a withered, tough, sinewy, steadfast people, perpetuating into our day the traditions of David and his kingdom. They are picturesque and heroic, these ancient sons of Judah. . . . But this community of scattered Jews has no significance for Palestine today or tomorrow. It is a survival, like the very deposits of the ancient *tels* [mounds] dug up these days by the archaeologist's pick and spade.

Secondly, there is the Christian community, . . . those religious orders which swarm in this historic land of the New Testament like locusts upon a wasted harvest field. . . . That most sacred of all places, the Church of the Holy Sepulchre, which should be the very sign and symbol of Christian unity, is *per contra* the raging center of confusion. There are other Christians in Palestine—the Templar settlements, the American colony, the Jerusalem Y.M.C.A., a few scattered schools and churches—welcome tokens that the religion of Jesus still survives, . . . but fringes, so to speak, upon the edge of a swamp of perverted and poisonous pietism. The Christian community of Palestine, as rooted deep in the soil of rival ecclesiasticisms, is a noisome and a noxious thing.

Thirdly, there is the Arab community, . . . the Middle Ages come to life again—the Moslem Middle Ages to be sure, but still the Middle Ages, . . . a society of poor, ignorant, supersti-

tious, toiling menials upon the land, and of proud, rich, idle
land-owners and nobility in the cities. . . . The Arabs in the
Holy Land are easily aroused by propaganda appeals to ignorance and superstition; but in essence they lie as inert today as
a thousand years ago, save as they have been touched, like the
dead bones of Ezekiel's vision, by the magic life of Zion! The
future of the Arab community in the Holy Land rests now
with their new Jewish brethren on the soil of Jezreel. This is
the new world of Palestine. And it is because the overlords of
Islam see this fact so clearly, that they fight so bitterly the . . .
alliance of Arab and Jew.

Lastly, there is the English community—important not to
Palestine but to Britain and the Empire. . . . There is in this
problem an entanglement of good and bad, of choice and necessity, of fate and freedom, which only the future, and hardly
this, can unravel. . . . From the standpoint of community life,
the English exist in Palestine as they exist in India, fundamentally as imperialists concerned with their dominant imperial
interests. Whatever the exigencies of the moment, the future
of Palestine, as of India, can be forecast only in terms of a
restoration of the country from rulers to people. The English
can exist in Palestine, in other words, only so long as an empire
can resist the steady advance of political and social democracy. . . . The English in Palestine are a community in the
Empire—yes! But not a community in the new Palestine of Zion!

The new Palestine of Zion! How inevitably this phrase drops
from the pen! For the new Palestine *is* Zion. Travel anywhere
in the Holy Land today, and wherever you touch the future as
distinguished from custom and tradition, life as distinguished
from decay and death, you find yourself in contact with these
heroic Jews who, gathered from many places, born of many
races, speaking many tongues, are yet welded together in the
heat of the one great passion for the restoration of Israel. . . .
These Zionists have a work to do, a life to develop, a soul to

quicken. And they have caught a vision which brings light at last into all the dark places of their ancestral inheritance. The old Jews, the Christians, the Arab *fellaheen*—these are the past; dead, or worse than dead! The English—these are of the present, and perhaps of the future, but a present and a future which are alien to all the interests of Palestine.

But the Zionists—these are of the real future. They live as a child lives, as a prophet lives, as God lives. They are life itself coming into ever greater and fairer bloom. They are the spirit engaged once more upon its old but ever new task of fresh creation. If Palestine lives today in its own beauty and by its own right, it is because the Zionists have made it live.

Through Gentile Eyes, 1938

THE GIFTS OF ZIONISM TO AMERICAN JEWRY

Speaking as a Gentile looking at my Jewish brethren here in our common country, I would say that we now see against the black background of European horror [1938] three things which Zionism has given to American Jewry:

First of all, it has given a *world consciousness.* Jews in this country are no longer separated from Jews in other countries in a selfish satisfaction with America as their own especial and favored destiny. In the quest of Zion they find themselves identified with Jews everywhere in working out a fulfillment of the Prophets' dream. . . . Thus is parochialism ended, and an Israel long scattered through the earth, like the severed limbs of Osiris, joined together again in the common organism of a common life. Zionism has given to the Jews what the Jews have not had since the destruction of Jerusalem—a united front . . . [in which] all [are] now primarily *Jews* in the rebuilding of the old waste places of the homeland which is their own again.

Secondly, Zionism has given to American Jews, as to all Jews everywhere, *a vision*. . . . What Israel has tragically lacked all these years has been a future to match its past. Through sheer force of ghastly circumstance, the Jews have been bound back onto the bondage of old days. To lay down their bones in the soil of Judaea was the hope that burned in many a tortured heart. . . . But now in Zionism came suddenly a future, a real future. The Jew was no longer a survivor merely from yesterday but a pioneer also of tomorrow. . . . Zionism was a vision which made life worth the living even amid humiliation, terror, and despair.

Lastly, Zionism has given to American Jews, as to all Jews, *a solution of their age-old problem*. What to do, save to flee one knows not whither—this has ever been the agony of Israel in Christendom! It is the one agony which could have made even more terrible the suffering of German Jews under the iron heel of Hitler. . . . But they had an answer to the question. The answer was—*Palestine!* They could send their children to that land of their fathers. They themselves, many of them, could go there and begin life anew. What was lost in the German Fatherland could be found again in the Jewish Homeland. . . . It was a goal which has not hitherto been seen, because it had not hitherto existed.

. . . The wonder of Zion is that the physical refuge on the map is a spiritual refuge within the soul. The homeland means a new self-respect, a nobler personal dignity, a self-reliance and courage and faith, for all Jews wherever they may be. The days of fawning and cringing are over. The days of adjustment and assimilation, of "escape," are likewise over. Jews now stand upon their feet, and look again the whole world in the face. For their problem is answered, and their destiny therefore secure. Herzl was the new Moses who ended the long period of Israel's second slavery by leading Israel again into the Promised Land.

Through Gentile Eyes, 1938

MARRIAGE AND DIVORCE

In most cases, it is simple honesty, to say nothing of morality and decency, to sever the marriage relation outwardly, when it has already been severed inwardly. I believe therefore in the granting of divorce, in order that a marriage may be ended legally, when it has already been ended morally. I believe that the process of divorce should be as solemn, and in many ways as difficult, as the original process of marriage. Special courts and magistrates should be provided for this process, which should have all the sanctity and privacy of the confessional; a rigid law should command a pause of time, for reconsideration and meditation, between the application for the divorce and its granting; every effort should be made to remove difficulties, reawaken love and a sense of responsibility, and thus to rehabilitate the family. But if, after all this has been done, the demand for a divorce is still insistent, society must consent.

Nor need we have any fear that the granting of divorces under these conditions will menace the stability of the family or threaten the integrity of the state. The essence of all true marriage, as we have said, is love—and love is the greatest thing in all the world! Let full freedom of choice be exercised in mating—let all worldly and material considerations as incentives to marriage be eliminated—let the union be protected and guaranteed by such regulations as we have laid down—let love be cherished and encouraged in every youthful heart, and then left to do its perfect work—and I believe that the instincts which have prompted the formation of the union may be safely trusted to safeguard its continuance. If these instincts of affection cannot cement the union for good and all, no legal reinforcements or restraints will ever avail. Spiritual ties, after all, are stronger than any that can be forged by legislatures or courts, and if these will not hold of their own divine strength, we might as well give up the fight. Love is our final resource, and I for one have no fear that it will ever wholly fail.

Marriage and Divorce, 1913

THE SHAME OF MAYOR WALKER'S NEW YORK

When as a man I look at the physical structure of New York and meditate upon this city as a business and cultural center, I am lifted up in sheer pride and exaltation. But when as a citizen I look upon the political conditions, I feel myself cast down in shame and humiliation. . . . It is altogether probable that when the lid, now being pried up with such enormous difficulty, has at last been lifted and the loathsome mess of corruption which festers beneath has been revealed to the light of day, the citizens of New York will rise up in their wrath and smite the persons responsible for the conditions which disgrace us. I shall myself not be at all surprised if in the end we see Mayor [James J.] Walker driven from office under the whip-lashes of the outraged conscience of the people. If he should thus fall, as others have fallen before, there would be a certain justice in his fate, for . . . he must yet be accused of high responsibility for the disgrace which has come upon this city during his administration. . . . Every one of us has the duty to indict him on at least three counts:

First, the Mayor of this city is guilty of neglecting his public duties and leaving them indifferently to the heedless care of incompetent or unworthy subordinates. . . . By his election to office Mr. Walker was charged with duties second only to those of the President of the United States, and these duties he has deliberately and wantonly neglected to the injury of the public health and the utter damage of his own political reputation.

Second, the Mayor of this city is guilty of acknowledging a

responsibility to a private political organization, Tammany Hall, which he recognizes as greater than his responsibility to the great public body of our citizenry. . . . That the voters of New York did not answer this cynical boast of public responsibility by driving the Mayor from office under the punishment of the heaviest political defeat ever administered to a candidate, I regard as one of the most shameful facts in the recent history of our community.

Lastly, the Mayor of this city is guilty of an insensitiveness to the moral corruption which now defames the city's name, as it degrades his own administration, which is as amazing as it is shocking. . . . The conduct of Mr. Walker in recent months demonstrates, if it demonstrates anything, that this man is devoid of conscience. He is as insensitive to public dishonor as a blind eye to fire or a deaf ear to noise. Whether he is to be pitied for his infirmity or condemned for his obtuseness, he still remains guilty of inexcusable betrayal of our city's good name and precious honor. . . .

The shame of Mayor Walker's New York is not the shame of Mayor Walker, not the shame of Tammany Hall, not the shame of corrupt judges and dishonest officials, bad as these are, but primarily the shame of a great body of citizens who have tolerated and consented to this situation for more years than I like to remember. Especially is the shame of New York to be found not so much in the great body of the citizens, who in their civic helplessness are more or less to be described as a flock of sheep, as in the outstanding leaders of this community who by education, ability, position, or power are inescapably charged with the responsibility of preserving the city's integrity and honor. I blame the shame of New York today primarily upon its financiers and bankers, its merchants, lawyers, physicians and clergymen, its educators, social workers and labor leaders, the hundreds of men and women who know so much about their government that they could save it if they would and yet care so little about it that they let it be looted beneath their very face and eyes. If the directors of a bank, or the trustees of a college or a church, were as careless of the integrity and welfare of their institutions as these business and professional leaders of New York are careless of the welfare and integrity of their city, they would be arrested, indicted, tried, convicted, and sent to jail. But let us not forget that, in the measure of our own responsibility, this shame belongs to us as well as to our civic leaders. We, the people, in the last analysis are responsible for the ills we suffer, and if we suffer them contentedly and without protest, must it not be agreed then after all we are getting only what we deserve!

. . . There must be organized within this city a permanent body of citizens of every church and party, of every class and creed, to stand watch and ward over the better life of our community.* It is for these things that I appeal to you, my fellow-citizens. And shall we not, as those who have now pondered upon these things, appeal as a single body to our fellow-citizens throughout the community whose welfare like our own is now at stake? . . . Will you not, therefore, join me in an appeal to all the people for the saving of our city? I present to you these resolutions which I ask you to heed and answer:

We, the congregation of the Community Church, and citizens of New York, alarmed and shocked by the evidence of corruption in the government of our city, do call upon the Governor of the state of New York, the Mayor of the city of New York, the several district attorneys, and all proper officers in authority among us, to use their every power under the law to expose and punish the wickedness in high places which is now sapping the life of our city and betraying the welfare of its people.

We appeal to our fellow-citizens in New York, more espe-

* Shortly thereafter, the City Affairs Committee was organized, with John Haynes Holmes as chairman and Stephen S. Wise as vice-chairman.

cially to financiers and businessmen, to lawyers, physicians and educators, to the pastors of our churches and the rabbis of our synagogues, to social workers, labor leaders, and all other leaders of public opinion, to join us in an organized movement for the revision of our municipal charter, to the end of delivering our city from political control and establishing it upon a non-partisan and scientific basis of administration.

And we, citizens of New York, do pledge ourselves this day to the single and loyal service of this great cause, that our city may at last become a safe abode of happy people and a monument to the integrity and security of our free democracy.

[*At the conclusion of the reading of these resolutions, the congregation rose to their feet with prolonged applause, then bowed their heads for the benediction upon their act of consecration.*]

> Sermon, "The Shame of Mayor
> Walker's New York,"
> *The Community Pulpit*, 1930

DEMOCRACY AND FREEDOM

In industry, exactly as in the church and in the state, it will need but a moment's peril to rob us all the freedom which we apparently had won. In Russia today we see a perfect instance of this fact. Here the revolution has taken place, and a vast new experiment in democracy is launched! Every true lover of progress desires this experiment to succeed. But almost from the beginning, liberty has broken down; and autocracy, by the deliberate choice of the men in control, has been lifted into its place. In other words, for the sake of democracy, as we are told, the tyranny of the Czar has been succeeded by the tyranny of the Bolsheviki. The revolutionists tell us that their power could not have been sustained and their work thus continued if they had trusted absolutely to the ideal principles of social freedom. This is undoubtedly true! But again we raise the question as to why, in order to protect liberty, this liberty should forthwith be abandoned? Here is a paradox which simply defies explanation! Such return to the practice of centralized authority may be justified, of course, in a hundred ways. It may be described as wise, prudent, necessary, inevitable. But one thing at least cannot be said of it, and that is that it is democratic! We may argue until "the crack of doom," but it will still remain indubitable that democracy is not democracy when liberty is overthrown. Some secret here is not yet solved. Some saving principle there is which we have not yet discovered. Democracy undoubtedly means at bottom the action of free men in a free world; but it is also something more and better than this, and it is this more and better that we must find.

New Churches for Old, 1922

THE SINS OF RADICALS

(1) If I were to name the sin which is more characteristic of radicals than any other—the one sin which embraces other sins, as the ocean embraces every sea—I would name the sin of *arrogance* or *pride*.

(2) We find ourselves face to face with another sin of the radicals when we see how arrogance develops into *dogmatism*.

(3) Another phase of this problem is presented, and another sin revealed, when we discover that most radicals are impervious to knowledge; they have *the closed mind*.

(4) A fourth sin, more serious than any of the others thus far named, [is] the sin of *intolerance*.

(5) Another sin, of which the radicals ought to be ashamed, [is] the sin of *uncharitableness*.

(6) The last indictment I want to bring against my radical brother is the charge that he, my brother, is himself *unbrotherly*, self-centered, exclusive, clannish, unwilling to have friends among the conservatives lest he betray his cause, [and] will not even join hands with other radicals.

Radicals have virtues that go far toward counter-balancing these failings of which we have spoken. Thus the radicals are idealists. Their interests are fundamentally spiritual and not material. They are living for a dream in the future and not for a reward in the present. They are willing to sacrifice comfort, security, reputation, sometimes life, for the sake of the dream they cherish in their hearts. They are thinking of humanity and not of themselves. They are unselfish, brave and steadfast. They are frequently disagreeable, hard to get along with, easy to criticize; yet, when all is said and done, they are today, as in all ages of the past, the one group of people in the world who meet the perfect test—"He that findeth his life, shall lose it; but he that loseth his life, shall find it."

The radicals, therefore, have their case. They are "the salt of the earth." But the salt may "lose its savor." And if it does, "it is thenceforth good for nothing, but to be cast down and trodden under foot." Take heed, therefore, my radical friends, ye that love and would serve this earth! For if the salt "hath lost its savor, wherewith shall it be salted?"

Sermon, *The Community Pulpit,*
1925

LIBERALS AND THE RUSSIAN REVOLUTION

In our enthusiasm over Russia's liberation from the Tsar [in 1917], in our excitement over the prospect of the future libera-

tion of the Russian people from economic as well as political
serfdom, in our vision of a new world springing from the womb
of Russia's travail, we liberals permitted ourselves to condone
wrongs that in our hearts we knew to be wrongs. We ignored
injustices and cruelties that under any other circumstances we
would have denounced. We consented to violations of principles that we knew to be fatal to the moral integrity of mankind. We defended, or at least apologized for, evils in the case
of Russia and atrocities by the Bolsheviki which horrified and
outraged us wherever else they appeared and by whomsoever
else they were done. Worst of all, many of us accepted tacitly,
if not openly—there is no other explanation of what we did!—
that most dangerous and ultimately disastrous idea that can
lodge within the human mind—namely, that the end justifies
the means. For the liberal, after all, is supposed to stand for
something that is intellectually and spiritually distinctive in our
civilization. If he is not faithful to a certain type of moral
idealism, what is his mission in the world?

The liberal's whole program, as I understand it, is a program
of humane methods directed to humane ends. His whole life
is rooted in an integrity which is itself rooted in liberty, enlightenment, and justice. He must serve the cause of freedom
and democracy without qualification, compromise, or adjustment; in the same way, only the other way 'round, he must
oppose tyranny and terror wherever they appear and by whatever argument they are defended. Above all, he must stand by
principle—the rigorous application of ideals of right and wrong.

If a liberal fails in any one of these particulars, he is no
longer a liberal. He is only one more of the fanatics on the Left
or the reactionaries on the Right who are shackled by prejudice
or passion to some temporary interest which is deemed greater
than eternal right. Yet it is just here that we liberals failed, and
therewith become enemies of our own appointed cause. We
abandoned, or suspended, in the case of Russia, those very

standards which are the structure of our faith. We tolerated, or excused, for Russia's sake, those very evils which are fatal to our life.

Sermon, "Why We Liberals Went
Wrong on the Russian Revolution,"
The Community Pulpit, 1939

FREE SPEECH

To hear a man attacking your most cherished beliefs, assailing those institutions which you regard as indispensable to social order and stability, and ridiculing your ideals and denouncing your activities—to hold in your hands the power to silence this man at any time, but to give him full opportunity to say what he wants to say, without interference or rebuke—this is to believe in free speech, and to be faithful to one's belief.

Editorial in *Unity,* 1921

V
THE HYMN WRITER

Once in a thousand years a call may ring
Divested so of every cumbering lie,
A man espousing it may fight and sing,
And count it but a little thing to die;
Once in a thousand years a star may come,
Six-pointed, tipped with such an astral flow,
Its singing sisters must bow hushed in dumb,
Half-mutinous, yet half-adoring show.

Once in as many years a man may rise
So cosmopolitan of thought and speech,
Humanity reflected in his eyes,
His heart a haven every race can reach,
That doubters shall receive a mortal thrust,
And own, "This man proves flesh exalts its dust."

> —COUNTEE CULLEN, "Millennial,"
> 1927, dedicated to John Haynes
> Holmes

THE ART OF THE HYMNIST

A hymn must be simple, . . . contain not the slightest suggestion of complexity, either of thought or of expression, . . . no unusual words, no fanciful figures of speech, no elaboration of diction or phrase. Those very devices of eloquence and beauty which the poet commands, as the composer commands the instruments in his orchestra, are here quite out of place. Simplicity is the word—simplicity, . . . the handmaid of clarity.

Secondly, a hymn must be characterized by feeling rather than by thought. It must appeal primarily to the heart, not to the mind, . . . stir and lift the soul, . . . comfort, challenge, and inspire.

Lastly, a hymn must draw its idea or theme from the familiar materials of life. . . . It may deal with great traditions of faith and hope and love, or mark transitions to new stages of spiritual apprehension, as in the social hymnology of our day. But always it must dwell where the heart of man is more or less at home. A hymn is a prayer, . . . the soul lifting itself from its daily lot to communion with the Most High. Therefore it must begin with what it knows, and only then reach out to what it dares to dream. . . .

The hymn-writer, dowered with any genuine gift, must . . . take these simple emotions of the heart, emotions that emerge from experiences of daily living interpreted as a quest for God, and express them in terms of simplicity, dignity, and exaltation of spirit. . . .

Hymns represent an art, a literary and spiritual art, as real as music, painting, or poesy, . . . a rare art, as delicate as the carving of ivory or the molding of chased gold.

"Hymns and Hymnists," in *The Collected Hymns of John Haynes Holmes*, 1960

IN NATURE'S TEMPLE VAST

Written at the Isles of Shoals, New Hampshire

O God, whose smile is in the sky,
   Whose path is in the sea,
Once more from earth's tumultuous strife
   We gladly turn to Thee.
Once more to Thee our songs we sing,
   Once more our prayers we raise,
And for the refuge of these isles
   Give Thee our deepest praise.

Here all the myriad sounds of earth
   In solemn stillness die,
While wind and wave unite to chant
   Their anthems to the sky;
Far, far away the heat and dust
   And panting of the race,
While here, in Nature's temple vast,
   We meet Thee face to face.

We come as those with toil far spent
   Who crave for rest and peace,
And from the care and fret of life
   Would find in Thee release;
We come as those who yearn to know
   The truth that makes men free;
And feel the love that binds us each
   To all, and all to Thee.

O Father, soothe all troubled thought,
   Dispel all idle fear,
Purge every heart of secret sin,
   And banish every care;

Until, as shine upon the seas
    The silent stars above,
There shines upon our trusting souls
    The light of Thine own love.

                1907

A HYMN OF TRUST

O God, whose law from age to age,
    No chance of change can know.
Whose love forevermore abides
    While aeons come and go;
From out the strife of earthly life
    To Thine embrace we flee,
And, 'mid our crowding doubts and fears,
    We put our trust in Thee.

The winds, Thy faithful messengers,
    Are guided by Thy hand;
Thy ministers, the flames of fire,
    Obey Thy stern command;
The seas resound within the bound
    Where Thy dominion reigns,
And wheeling planets seek the paths
    The cosmic will ordains.

Thy steadfast purpose moves before
    The nations on their way,
And guides the stumbling hosts of men
    From darkness into day.
The prophet's word, the captain's sword,
    The judge's rod and rood,
Lead through the patience of the years
    Until the goal of good.

Eternal, we would learn to trust
   The doing of Thy will,
And in Thy spirit's constancy
   Our doubts and fears would still.
Help us to know, in joy or woe,
   In ease or race hard-run,
That Thou, the Universal Life,
   In law and love art one.

1910/1931

THE VOICE OF GOD

The voice of God is calling
   Its summons unto men;
As once he spake in Zion,
   So now he speaks again:
Whom shall I send to succor
   My people in their need?
Whom shall I send to loosen
   The bonds of shame and greed?

I hear my people crying
   In cot and mine and slum;
No field or mart is silent,
   No city street is dumb.
I see my people falling
   In darkness and despair.
Whom shall I send to shatter
   The fetters which they bear?

We heed, O Lord, Thy summons,
   And answer: Here are we!
Send us upon Thine errand!
   Let us Thy servants be!

Our strength is dust and ashes,
   Our years a passing hour;
But Thou canst use our weakness
   To magnify our power.

From ease and plenty save us,
   From pride of place absolve;
Purge us of low desire,
   Lift us to high resolve.
Take us and make us holy,
   Teach us Thy will and way;
Speak, and behold we answer!
   Command, and we obey!

1913

ANNIVERSARY HYMN

Written on the occasion of the tenth anniversary of becoming minister of the Church of the Messiah, New York City

O Thou, whose presence moved before
The darkly wandering tribes of yore,
Whose steadfast purpose, like a star,
Looked down on nations from afar;

Thou God, whose living voice was heard
In psalmist's song, and prophet's word,
Whose holy will turned kings to dust,
And glorified the martyrs' trust;

Eternal God, who blessed our sires,
When here they lit their altar fires,
And raised with them this sacred dome,
Where now Thou makest still Thy home;

To us, dear Lord, this latter day
Send out Thy light upon our way;
Lift high Thy spirit's pillared flame
Above our wilderness of shame.

This temple makes an ark of grace,
Where we may meet Thee face to face;
This shrine an altar fair and tall,
Whence sounds the thunder of Thy call.

And lo, Thy people, now as then,
Will seek Thy Promised Land again,
And stay not, till in fields untrod,
Is built the Kingdom of our God.

1917

INTERNATIONAL HYMN

O'er continent and ocean,
    From city, field and wood,
Still speak, O Lord, Thy messengers
    Of peace and brotherhood.
In Athens and Benares,
    In Rome and Galilee,
They fronted kings and conquerors,
    And taught mankind of Thee.

We hear, O Lord, these voices,
    And hail them as Thine own;
They speak as speak the winds and tides
    On planets far and lone:
One God, the life of Ages;
    One Rule, His Will above;

One realm, our wide Humanity;
   One Law, the Law of Love.

The tribes and nations falter
   In rivalries of fear,
The fires of hate to ashes turn,
   To dust, the sword and spear.
Thy word alone remaineth;
   That word we speak again,
O'er sea and shore and continent,
   To all the sons of men.

1917

BEHOLD, O GOD, OUR HOLY HOUSE

Written on the occasion of the burning of the Church of the Messiah (the Community Church) on September 11, 1919. The hymn was sung at the union services held by All Souls (Unitarian) Church of New York on the following Sunday, September 18.

Behold, O God! our holy house
   And beautiful is burned;
The altars by our fathers reared
   To dust and ashes turned.

We stand as those who, driven far
   By waste of fire and sword,
Find not in unfamiliar ways
   The presence of the Lord.

But lo, through storm and flame there fly
   Words wing'd of faith and love;
Quick to our sudden need are friends,
   Like angels from above.

This strange and crowded world becomes
    One vast cathedral fair;
And every humblest heart of man,
    An altar for our prayer.

We have Thee, Lord. Our house is dust,
    But Thou art living still
Within the loved community
    Of souls that do Thy will.

                    1919

WITNESS BORN ON JUDAH'S HILLS

Dedicated to Rabbi Stephen S. Wise and the Free Synagogue
in New York City, and sung on April 17, 1932, for the first time,
at the service commemorating the twenty-fifth anniversaries of
the founding of the congregation and the beginning of Dr.
Wise's rabbinate in that pulpit in 1907.

The flames of Sinai clothe no more
    The presence of the Lord;
The desert winds no echoes bear
    Of Moses' thund'rous word;
Yet still in wildernesses far
    Moves Israel's chosen band,
Resolv'd through want and waste and woe
    To find the Promised Land.

Dust unto dust, Hosea's bones
    Lie deep in Zion's sod;
The ashes of the centuries hide
    The stones Isaiah trod;
Yet still on Israel's altars burn
    The fires of prophecy,

And lips with living coals are touched
   The doom of sin to cry.

O God of Israel, not in vain
   Thy sons proclaimed Thy law;
The witness born on Judah's hills
   Holds still a world in awe;
And lo, today in this far land,
   In him, Thy servant true,
In these Thy people, strong and free,
   Thy spirit lives anew.

1932

THE PURPOSE HIGH

Written on the occasion of the twenty-fifth anniversary of becoming minister of the Community Church of New York.

Great Spirit of the speeding spheres,
Whose constant orbits mark the years,
Whose tides arise, then flow apart,
As pulse-beats of the cosmic heart,

Thou God, to Whom an aeon gone
Is but as yesterday when done,
The centuries' march of tribe and clan
The shadow of a moment's span;

How canst Thou know our transient days?
Why shouldst Thou trace our trivial ways?
Why hold within Thine awful hand
These motes of dust, these grains of sand?

Yet we are Thine! Th' eternal flood
Flows through the currents of our blood,

Th' undying fire of star and sun
Kindles our souls, and makes them one.

One with Thy life, ere time began,
Nor knew the rise and fall of man;
One till the numbered years are fled,
And earth to cold and darkness sped!

Teach us, O God, the purpose high
Which moves the spaces of the sky,
That our quick day, from error free,
May live in Thine eternity.

1932

TO MAKE US ONE IN THEE

Thou God of all, whose spirit moves
   From pole to silent pole;
Whose purpose binds the starry spheres
   In one stupendous whole;
Whose life, like light, is freely poured
   On all men 'neath the sun;
To Thee we lift our hearts, and pray,
   That Thou wilt make us one.

One in the patient company
   Of those who heed Thy will,
And steadfastly pursue the way
   Of Thy commandments still;
One in the holy fellowship
   Of those who challenge wrong,
And lift the spirit's sword to shield
   The weak against the strong.

One in the truth that makes men free,
The faith that makes men brave;
One in the love that suffers long
To seek, and serve, and save;
One of the vision of Thy peace,
The Kingdom yet to be—
When Thou shalt be the God of all,
And all be one in Thee.

1946

VI

L'ENVOI

The others move. The other stars wheel by.
Inching across the night, they saunter forth.
But this one mental fire stays sternly north,
Unhindered by the drift across the sky.

A compass will be set against this light
In later years, when ships are planned to scar
Pale glimmering waters, formerly too far,
And undiscovered countries loom in sight.

There must be movement as the planets press
Their plea for music, rhythmical design,
But man's unsteady heart will choose as shrine
A polar point of astral changelessness.

—EDITH LOVEJOY PIERCE,
dedicated to J.H.H., 1939

I SPEAK FOR MYSELF

I have never surrendered my mind to any church, or party, or individual yet, and I do not propose to begin now. I have ever counted it my highest duty, as well as my most precious privilege, to do my own thinking, reach my own opinions, stand by my own convictions—and I shall try to remain faithful to that duty to the end. For I was raised in a tradition which seems to be unfamiliar to this age. I was taught early in my life that one must be true to oneself—that independence of ideas and ideals was essential to dignity and self-respect—that Emerson was right when he said that "who would be a man must be a non-conformist." Nothing to me is quite so intolerable as running with the crowd, lining up with the church or the party, licking up the dust before the feet of the great leader.

> Statement on occasion of his
> retirement, 1949, as quoted in
> *The Christian Register*,
> September 20, 1954

CHRISTIANITY'S DEBT TO JUDAISM

Christianity owes a heavy debt to Judaism. Christianity ought to be willing to recognize and pay this debt, as any honorable debtor recognizes and pays his obligation.

That pure religion and undefiled which sprang from the heart of Jesus was propagated far and wide by his disciples and apostles, was recorded in the pages of the New Testament, and remains to this day the greatest single spiritual influence in human history. This religion is in reality Jewish in origin and content. It is only an accident that it did not remain in the end what it was in the beginning—a part and parcel of the Jewish world. Now that it is one of the separate religions of mankind, its patronage should be confessed, and its heritage duly honored.

In spirit as well as in blood, the Nazarene, Jesus, was a son of Israel. It is to the Jews that the Christians owe this peerless leader and founder of their faith. His rightful place in history is that of the last and greatest of the Jewish prophets.

The Bible, the sacred Scriptures of the Christian church, consists of two parts—the Old Testament, so called, and the New. The Old Testament, which comprises some three-fourths of the Bible, belongs not to Christianity at all but to Judaism. The Old Testament, let it be said, is the Jewish Bible!

The Old Testament is not Christian. It is Jewish through and through; and whenever we use it we should remember that we are turning to Jewish sources for instruction and inspiration.

As for the New Testament, this is our own. But even so, it is only fair to recognize that the New Testament is throughout a Jewish book. Every word of it, from the first chapter of Matthew to the last chapter of Revelation, was written by Jews, and thus is saturated with the Jewish spirit and ideals.

Next to the Bible comes the church—by which I mean not the hierarchy, which belongs to a later period of history, but the simple fact of the congregation of men and women meeting together on a Sunday morning for the worship of Almighty God. Where did this reality come from? Why, from the Jews— more specifically, from that generation of Jews which suffered the tragic experience of the Exile [in 586 B.C.].

The synagogue became as well recognized an institution of Judaism as the Temple itself, and held in time the first devotion of the people. Jesus knew the synagogue of Nazareth from his youth up, and in this synagogue began his ministry. When, following his death, his followers carried on his work, it was first in synagogues, and only later in churches of their own, that they proclaimed the Gospel. But these churches, when they came, were modeled precisely on Jewish example and thus were the daughters of the synagogue. When Christians meet today on Sunday mornings to worship God and to consecrate their lives to His service, and to preserve the sacred traditions of the faith, they are doing not only what the early Christians did, but what the Jews have done since the sad days of the Exile. We have a church because the Jews first had a synagogue. The former is the direct descendant of the latter.

In addition to the Bible and the church is Sunday as the sacred day of rest and worship—the one day in seven set scrupulously aside for purposes of physical recreation and spiritual regeneration. Where did this Christian Sunday come from? Why, obviously, from the Jewish Sabbath. It is true that the Jewish Sabbath is the last day of the week—traditionally the day when God rested from his labors after the six days of the Creation. The Christian Sunday, in contrast, is the first day of the week, so celebrated because it was on this first day that Jesus is supposed to have risen from the dead. So the first day among the Christians came to take the place of the seventh day among Jews. But this detail is unimportant. The central fact is that the Christian Sunday is the rebirth of the Jewish Sabbath—the Christian once again taking his religious practices from the Jew!

What about the teachings of Christianity—those great truths of the moral and spiritual life which constitute the essence of the Gospel? The things which Jesus taught—were those original with him, or did they spring from the Judaism in which Jesus was born and reared? In his ministry [Jesus was] not practicing a new religion, but reviving the pure and undefiled religion of Israel! Not starting a movement of revolt against Judaism, but only a movement of reform inside of Judaism! Not forsaking the Jewish synagogue and starting the Christian church, but cleansing the Jewish synagogue. Nothing would have surprised Jesus more than to have learned after his death that his work had led to a new religion largely hostile to his own. To this day he would not have understood the meaning of Christianity and Christian doctrine.

Jesus was a Jew, in the great traditions of the Prophets. He aw a religion in his time, as Isaiah and Amos and Jeremiah ad seen a religion in their time, which had become overlaid and encrusted with a vast growth of theological and ecclesiastical literalism which was fatal to the pure essence of the faith. All this he sought to sweep away. "The letter killeth, but the spirit giveth life!" The Nazarene wanted to find that spirit again. Therefore did he seek, like the shepherd his lost sheep, that great body of Jewish prophecy which was the real religion of Israel. So everything that was precious in Judaism came to life again in Jesus. He was teaching what was truest and noblest in the tradition of his own people. He sought for nothing but the restoration of Israel to its true faith.

Such is the debt which Christianity owes to Judaism! Not Jesus merely, nor the Bible, the church and Sunday, but the whole substance of Christian teaching!

The debt must be acknowledged, somewhat as I have tried to acknowledge it. Why should not Christians everywhere recognize Jesus as a Jew? Why should they not have the grace to refer to the Old Testament, when they use it, as "the Jewish Scriptures"? Why should they not acclaim the kinship of the church with the synagogue, and of the Christian Sunday with the Jewish Sabbath? As for the Gospel, what would be lost and what not gained, if the Jewish sources of this teaching were at last made plain? Why may we not pay this debt to the Jews by fighting anti-Semitism? All around us rages this noisome and fatal plague. It works its havoc not merely in Germany and Europe, but right here in America. Half-hidden, half-confessed, whispered rather than shouted, taking shape not in hideous persecutions but in countless little irritations and injustices, but none the less fatal as a prejudice which poisons the soul, this curse—as it is—is Christianity's curse, and it should be ended for very shame. Here the church, in the very name of Jesus, should take the lead in stamping out this pestilence that devours ourselves as well as our victims. To fight and destroy anti-Semitism—this would be a large payment on the debt.

To bring Jews and Christians together, not by converting or merging one with the other, but by recognition of that spiritual kinship which makes them one—this is our holy task. To end the injustice and horror of the ages in finding and binding that "unity of the spirit which is the bond of peace"! Already Jews and Christians are one in all that is central to the outer relations of our lives? In both branches of the severed family there rests the obligation to shake off separation and end isolation, but most heavily and immediately does this obligation rest upon Christians, who have the numbers, the power—and this debt which must be paid!

Sermon, *The Community Pulpit,*
1946

WHERE JUDAISM IS SUPERIOR
TO CHRISTIANITY

Judaism is superior to Christianity, first of all, in its emphasis upon the moral law. Whereas Christianity is inclined to be concerned primarily with matters of theological belief, Judaism does not hesitate to be concerned primarily with matters of ethical precept and example. As the one exalts the ideal of faith, so the other exalts the ideal of conduct. What the creed is sup-

posed to mean to the Christian, the tables of the law are supposed to mean to the Jew. It is in the Jewish emphasis upon
morality, as compared with the Christian emphasis upon theology, that I see the first superiority of the religion of the synagogue over the religion of the church. Turn to your Old
Testament and note the infinite refinements of the Jewish law
giving way to the poetry of the Psalms and the moral passion of
the Prophets. Then turn to your New Testament and note the
pure, transcendent spiritual idealism of Jesus rapidly swallowed
up in the theological logic-chopping of St. Paul.

If I would sum up all that Judaism has meant to itself and
to the world, since the days of its earliest spiritual power, I
would speak the single, mighty word: "Righteousness." What
Christianity has meant in this one distinctive way, I am not
ready now to say, but it is not "Righteousness." Or if, at certain
times, it has meant "Righteousness," as in the days of the
Calvinistic reforms in Geneva, or the Puritan revolution in
England, its inspiration thereto has come not from the New
Testament but from the Old. Nothing is more significant in the
history of the Christian world than the fact that every moral
revival has been accompanied by a new discovery of the Old
Testament. It is from the Jews that the moral idealism of the
race has come; and in so far as this idealism is central to the
problem of human life upon this earth, I affirm that Judaism
is superior to Christianity.

A second point of superiority of Judaism over Christianity
is to be found in the fact that Judaism is concerned with life
upon this side of the grave, whereas Christianity is predomi-
nantly concerned with life upon the other side of the grave.
Judaism emphasizes present need and responsibility; Christianity emphasizes future hope and experience. Judaism is interested
in the fact that "now are we the Sons of God"; Christianity is
perplexed by the fact that "it doth not yet appear what we
shall be." It is in this emphasis upon the realities of this present

life, that we find Judaism perhaps most sharply distinguished from Christianity.

This does not mean that Judaism has no belief in immortality. Among all the practices of church and synagogue, I know of nothing more touching than the prayer of mourning for "the loss of loved ones" that is spoken regularly on every Sabbath evening in the religious services of the Jews. As the noble call is spoken, there arise those who mourn their dead, and they listen in comfort to the sweet assurance that "only the body has died and has been laid in the dust. The spirit lives and will live forever in the shelter of God's love and mercy." But not the least impressive feature of this prayer is the immediate reminder to the mourners of "this life, also," and of the memory of the dead as "an incentive to conduct by which the living honor the dead." It is as though the Jews could not think of the life beyond except in terms of the life that now is.

The whole religion of Christianity, we may say, is a system of salvation for a future life. Remove this element from the texture of Christian faith, and you would have nothing left; just as you would have nothing left in Judaism if you should wipe out the vision of the day when "the Lord will cause righteousness and peace to spring forth before all nations." In this interpretation of the Kingdom of God by the Jews as an ideal society of righteousness and peace set up here upon the earth, and the contrasting interpretation of the Kingdom of God by the Christians as a heavenly society set up in the spirit world beyond the grave, we find the fundamental difference between Judaism and Christianity.

I hold Judaism to be superior to Christianity, in the third place, because it emphasizes society as contrasted with the characteristic Christian emphasis upon the individual. Judaism sees the group, Christianity the separate person. It is in this recognition of the common life, as contrasted with the typical Christian recognition of the single life, that I see an immense

superiority of Judaism over Christianity. We are saved together, in other words, or we are not saved at all. The very fact
of living together, in the communion of the common life, is
itself our heaven; as the fact of living not together, but apart
in selfish isolation, is itself our hell. Whether by temperament,
training, or sheer historical accident, the Jews have laid hold
upon this truth, and made it central in their social, political and
religious life. They think, as a kind of instinct, apparently, not
of themselves but of their tribe. If the tribe suffers, they must
suffer; if the tribe dies, then they must die; if the tribe is saved,
then, and then alone, can they be saved. "Be not wroth very
sore, O Lord, neither remember iniquity forever; behold, see,
we beseech thee, *we are all Thy people.*" This is the age-old
cry of the Jews—Thy people, Lord, Thy people!—and this is
the cry of religion in the highest and noblest sense of the word.
In so far as we, in this Community Church, deliberately make
this cry of the common life our own, we are much more of a
synagogue than we are of a church. And of this, may I say, I
am not ashamed, but *proud!*

It is in these three points that Judaism is to be rated superior
to Christianity. We are finding Judaism in many respects to
be nearer to the heart of true religion than Christianity.

Sermon, *The Community Pulpit,*
1928

WHERE CHRISTIANITY IS SUPERIOR
TO JUDAISM

(1) I deem Christianity to be superior to Judaism in the fact
that it possesses Jesus as "the author and finisher of [its] faith."
I have in mind a man, born as other men are born, imperfect
even as we are imperfect, dowered with no other than human

powers, slain before he had reached any maturity of wisdom or fullness of experience, and yet the noblest personal embodiment of religious idealism that the world has ever seen. Other religions have great leaders—Moses, Confucius, Buddha, Zoroaster, Mohammed—but no one of them has that transcendent quality which is so apparent in Jesus as almost to persuade us of his divinity. In his name, [Christianity] can speak, in his life it can live, in his person it can commend itself to men. When creeds are forgotten and churches are crumbled into dust, Christianity will remain a power upon the earth, because the world will never be willing to forget the Nazarene. There is simply nothing in Judaism to compare with Jesus, excepting Jesus himself, this Jewish youth cast out of the synagogue in which he was born and reared, and rejected ever since by his own brethren. The Jews should recapture Jesus. They should do this not merely for themselves, that they may possess again what once belonged to them, but also for Jesus, that he may be delivered from the extraneous entanglements of myth and dogma in which he has been lost for centuries, and thus restored to the essential simplicity and beauty of his Jewish inheritance.

(2) The second superiority of Christianity over Judaism is an interpretation of moral idealism higher than any that preceded it, and marking, I believe, the highest insight ever attained into the problem of human living. *Love,* service for others' sakes, laying down one's life for a friend, this is the new, the greater, the higher righteousness. It is a new epoch which can prompt the cry "Love is the fulfilling of the law."

(3) Christianity is in spirit and purpose at least a universal religion, whereas Judaism is a religion of a nation and a people. It is this failure of Jesus, as his contemporaries put it, and as most Jews would put it today, or, as I would prefer to put it, this refusal of Jesus, to see and respect the nationalistic aspects of Judaism, which constitutes the third and most conspicuous superiority of Christianity. Judaism has a political and racial

as well as a religious significance. The Jews are first of all, perhaps, a people, and only secondarily a group of worshipers.
[Their] prophets dreamed of a united world—the ending of
war and dissension in a brotherhood of man—but it was always
in terms of other nations being "joined with the house of
Jacob." The Jews, after all, were a chosen people—they had a
special mission—they must not lose themselves in the encom-
passing body of humanity. The danger of absorption was great
in the midst of the mightier peoples who surrounded them. The
danger has been great ever since in the dispersion among alien
and hostile tribes throughout the world. [The Jews'] racial integrity is one of the miracles, as it is one of the hero-sagas, of
history. But it is a movement of separatism all the same, and
thus an occasion for division among mankind.

Christianity, if true to itself, knows nothing of race, or nation,
or social class. It reaches out to the farthest bounds of human
habitation upon the earth; it reaches down to the lowest depths
of human need within society. Christianity is universal or it is
nothing. To identify it with the political destiny of a nation,
and thus with patriotism, is to betray its mission and to destroy
its life. To mingle it with prejudice against any group of men
of any race or any religion, is to poison the springs of its influence at their very source. To set it apart from any human
interest among any class of men in any part of the world, is
to crucify Christ again upon Mt. Calvary. Jesus died for men,
for *all* men. Christianity can be true to him, and to itself, only
as it lives for men, for *all* men. This is its duty—and its glory!

Sermon, *The Community Pulpit,*
1928

THE RELIGION SUPERIOR TO BOTH
JUDAISM AND CHRISTIANITY

Judaism is imperishable, as great art is imperishable. I do not wonder that millions still find in it the "living sources" of their faith.

In the same way is Christianity imperishable; it has made contributions to the task of human living which can never be forgotten or ignored.

But time has not ended. Progress has not ceased. "God is not dumb that he should speak no more." Neither is man dead that he should strive no more to widen his vision and deepen his experience. With neither Judaism nor Christianity can the soul of man stand still. The course of evolution is as inevitable in the world of spirit as in the world of matter. The same thing must be said of those today who would stay the development of religion with the word either of Moses or of Jesus. What these geniuses revealed in Law and Gospel is permanent, and must remain forever in the spiritual consciousness of men. But what they revealed is not final; new experience must ever bring new revelations of truth.

This evolutionary process makes it inevitable that a new and greater religion should develop out of the old, that new and greater forms of life should develop out of those which have gone before, a religion which itself will be evolutionary, an unfolding, enlarging, ever-changing form of spiritual experience which will stop with no revelations or discoveries but move ever onward with the unceasing progress of the race.

In the ever-moving, ever-enlarging vision of the soul, we have a religion that escapes finalities, [a] religion superior to both Judaism and Christianity. As Judaism, from the standpoint of time, has its finality in Moses, so also, from the standpoint of space, it has its bounds within the house of Jacob. In the same way as Christianity has its finality in Christ, so also it has its bounds within the church of Christ. But here is a religion, in suggestion at least, which has its bounds in nothing short of the horizon of the world. For this religion is concident with human experience.

[I anticipate] a religion which will recognize all religions to be true as so many precious deposits of the spiritual experience of man, and which will accept all religions as divine in the exact measure of their faith and vision. If Mohammedanism is a way of life and a method of salvation for millions of believers, then is Mohammedanism, for them at least, a true religion. If Hinduism brings inspiration and spiritual guidance to myriads of honest men and women, and furnishes strength and solace to even one such soul as Mahatma Gandhi, then is Hinduism to be reverenced as a pathway to the Eternal. These Mohammedans and Hindus and other pagans (so called) need not become Christians in order to be saved. No longer is there distinction between paganism on the one side and the one true faith of Christ or Moses upon the other. Religions are many, says the familiar adage, but religion is one. Religions are many as the parts of one basic and all-inclusive religion, as the branches of a tree are many, as the parts of a single race of mankind. In the spirit, as in the body, we are one; and one therefore is the faith by which we live.

The new religion is a religion not of theology but of science. This does not mean the abandonment of religion to materialism, as so many of our contemporaries seem to fear. It is true that we must take the material facts of life as the basis of all knowledge. We must sit at the feet of the astronomers, and chemists, and biologists, and learn from them the realities of existence. Especially from them must we learn the method and the spirit of their inquiry. But this is only the beginning of our work. What science gives is but the raw material, out of which to build the structure of spiritual faith. It is the fabric out of which to weave the pattern of spiritual vision.

We are not leaving spiritual reality behind when we turn from scriptures and creeds and holy laws; nor are we abandoning ourselves to materialism when we profess an interest in atoms and molecules and evolving processes of organic life. Such distinction, I say, is false! What we have here, in this development of scientific interest, is the distinction not between things spiritual and material, but the distinction rather between things true and untrue. What we are learning today, if we be honest, is the sober fact that what Judaism and Christianity have been believing about the world and man, through all these centuries gone by, is simply false, a great mass of traditional ideas which are erroneous in the sense that they have no basis in reality. Science is showing us the truth, and how to find the truth. And it is because the new religion of our time is accepting from science what science is alone competent to teach, that I regard this religion as superior to both Judaism and Christianity.

Sermon, *The Community Pulpit,*
1928

TO DONALD SZANTHO HARRINGTON

[Donald Harrington came to the Community Church in 1944 as Junior Colleague. In 1949 he succeeded Holmes as Senior Minister.]

Words of welcome, September 24, 1944:

. . . I am mindful of the precious gifts which Mr. Harrington is to bring to me, a battered veteran of more than forty years of service, who is in sore need of them. Energy, courage, initiative, ambition, enthusiasm untouched by disappointment, idealism unspoiled by dark experience, abundant hope, triumphant faith—these are the things which he is going to give me. I can accept them easily and happily, especially in the memory of that day, more than thirty-seven years ago, when I was received into this pulpit by an older man, Dr. Robert Collyer, then Pastor Emeritus of this church. There were fifty-six years between his age and mine, as there are thirty-five years, Don, between my age and yours. To my dying day I shall remember the love with which Dr. Collyer embraced me, the wisdom with which he guided me, the tenderness with which he gave me comfort and reassurance. I cannot give you these precious things, for such benefactions spring only from the greatest souls. But what I can give you, Don, in whatsoever measure, I promise to give you. Here and now I pledge you all I have and all I am, and I want you to know that so long as I am spared to serve this church, which in the nature of things cannot now be many years, I shall make it my prayer both day and night that never, even in the smallest things, may I fail to serve you.

But I must give you welcome, Don, not only for myself but for the people of this great congregation as well. . . . This is the most heterogeneous aggregation of people that you ever saw in your life. You will find in this company all kinds of Christians from Catholics to Quakers. There are many Jews— not so many today as usual, for these are the holy days, and our Jewish friends insist upon running away to their synagogues! And there are representatives of other religions, and of no religion at all. Here are believers and unbelievers, conservatives and radicals, men and women of all nationalities and of all races. We are a great and diverse company. And if we hold together at all, it is not because we seek any identity of opinion or attitude, but rather because we have learned to accept the principle of freedom, to practice the virtues of tolerance and good will, and to understand that religion means that we shall have love one for another. Thus are we joined in that "unity of the spirit which is the bond of peace." . . .

I rejoice to think of the love that these people are going to bestow upon you, Don. It has been my happy experience to enjoy this love through all these years gone by, and I know what it is. Now you are to have it. And the beauty of it is that in giving their love to you, these people take none of it away from me. For love is like light—with one candle-flame we kindle another, and as the second burns, the first is undiminished.

. . . We receive you with confidence and love, knowing that as we are to be one with you, so you are ever to be one with us.

Words of installation, November 19, 1944:

My dear Harrington, as beloved to my soul as a son to my flesh, your decision this day to renew with us your solemn ordination of five years ago lifts up our hearts with joy. There is not a soul within this place who does not feel strengthened and inspired by your entrance upon the ministry of this church in this dread hour of history. You come to serve us at a time when we need the freshness of your youth, the unspoiled ardor of your faith, the undimmed vision of your pure heart. We welcome you as those who are eager to answer when you call, and follow where you lead. We have confidence in you just because we see you dare to face, with the bare weapon of the spirit, the scene that now confronts the world; and we have confidence in the church, *our* church, because you choose to use it as the instrument of your life's devotion to mankind. Not in years has this church been so happy, and so reassured, as in this event of your installation when we look into your calm, strong face, feel the beat of your warm, stout heart, and realize that you are ours, as we are yours, and that together, at an hour not too late, we may struggle to save humanity from death.

Behold a cloud of witnesses surrounding us this day—the dead who have died, in ages gone, for what we now would live! Shall we not here highly resolve that these dead shall not have died in vain, that this world, under God, shall have a new birth of freedom, and that the government of his Kingdom shall not perish from the earth.

Words of consecration to his successor, March 28, 1949:

Don, this is a solemn moment in my life. I am surrendering, on the eve of the Psalmist's span of years, my most precious possession. Like Cornelia, the Roman matron, who, when asked to show her jewels, presented her two sons, Tiberius and Gaius, so I present my jewels, this congregation, which I can keep no longer. It is grievous for me to give these people up. But my comfort is that I am placing them in your tender and loving care. . . . So does life run its blessed course, with no regret, but always with exceeding great joy.

The Community Pulpit,
1944/1949

NEO-ORTHODOXY

The so-called Neo-Orthodox theologians of our time I would condemn and criticize as presenting the worst instead of the best in human nature, for to them man is a monstrous creature. He knows his sinful condition, and knows, also, his utter inability to do anything about it. The result is an incurable wickedness which overcomes all virtue. It is damnation come again, with our World Wars the dreadful witness of man's plight. That a theology of this kind can long survive is not to be believed. It may seem to flourish for a time, especially under conditions such as prevail today. It may leave in its wake a litter of queer and sterile faiths, as witnessed by the poisonous cult of Immoralism. But in the end the true spirit of man will assert itself and save the world anew.

Editorial in *Community News,*
February, 1956

A RE-APPRAISAL

I am convinced that, in this age of wreck and ruin, of despair and death, man himself is still undefeated. If he is baffled, it is to fight better; if he has fallen, it is to rise. The fabric of one more dream has crashed to ruin—this civilization has seen, or must soon see, its end. But the travail of this hour is the travail at once of birth as well as of death. Even as it perishes, it produces Einstein, Freud, Lenin, Gandhi—four geniuses of mind and spirit greater than any four who have yet appeared in any single age. They read the signs of the times; they point the farther way. In their words and deeds we see as it were the seeds of undying life sprouting like the grain of wheat in the crumbling hand of the Egyptian mummy. In their ideas and labors we hear as it were the tones of prophecy that not only proclaim but promise the time to come. What awaits us we cannot know. But if another world declines and falls, and another thousand years of the Dark Ages intervene, we need not fear. Here in this creative thought and sacrificial spirit, there is Life at work.

If not today, nor tomorrow, nor yet the day after tomorrow, then in some more remote but certain time, man will solve his problem and secure his life. And meanwhile we must fight on undaunted for the right, trusting that final victory which we may surely serve but ourselves shall scarcely see.

In an older time, there was a day like this. The empire of all the world had fallen. Into Rome itself had entered the hordes of barbarians. Across the seas, in Hippo, there sat the immortal bishop of that African city. As darkness lowered ever blacker upon his day, he lifted up his eyes, and saw in vision the city of God. While the destroyers of the empire were drawing near, he wrote the voluminous pages of that treatise wherein he designed the plan and pattern of that Eternal City. And he believed that that City would be built, and built upon, until the dreams of all men's hearts should be at last fulfilled. And even as the invaders hammered upon the gates of Hippo, to break them to the ground, St. Augustine wrote his closing word: "How great shall that felicity be, where shall be no evil thing, where no good thing shall lie hidden, and where we shall have leisure to utter forth the praises of God, which shall be all in all!"

> Berry Street Conference Address, May Meetings of the American Unitarian Association, Boston, as quoted in *The Christian Register*, July 19, 1934

AVE ATQUE VALE

From Life to Death!
An eager breath,
A battle for the true and good,
An agony upon the rood;
A dark'ning of the light—
And night!

From Death to Life!
A peace from strife;

A voyage o'er an ocean wide
That moves from shore to shore its tide;
  A passing of the night—
    And light!

1910

THE WRITINGS OF
JOHN HAYNES HOLMES

(*in chronological order*)

The Old and the New. Privately printed, Dorchester, Mass., 1906.

The Revolutionary Function of the Modern Church. New York:
G. P. Putnam's Sons, 1912.

Marriage and Divorce. New York: B. W. Huebsch, 1913.

Is Death the End? New York: G. P. Putnam's Sons, 1915.

New Wars for Old. New York: Dodd, Mead and Co., 1916.

Religion for Today. New York: Dodd, Mead and Co., 1917.

The Life and Letters of Robert Collyer, Vols. I and II. New York:
Dodd, Mead and Co., 1917.

Readings from Great Authors (co-editor). New York: Dodd, Mead
and Co., 1918.

The Grail of Life (co-editor). New York: Dodd, Mead and Co.,
1919.

Is Violence the Way Out? New York: Dodd, Mead and Co., 1920.

New Churches for Old. New York: Dodd, Mead and Co., 1922.

Patriotism Is Not Enough. New York: Greenberg Publishers, Inc.,
1925.

Palestine Today and Tomorrow. New York: The Macmillan Co.,
1929.

The Heart of Scott's Poetry. New York: Oxford University Press,
1932.

The Sensible Man's View of Religion. New York: Harper and
Brothers, 1932.

If This Be Treason (with Reginald Lawrence). New York: The
Macmillan Co., 1935.

Through Gentile Eyes. New York: Jewish Opinion Publishing
Corp., 1938.

Rethinking Religion. New York: The Macmillan Co., 1938.

Out of Darkness. New York: Harper and Brothers, 1942.

The Second Christmas and Other Stories. New York: The Macmillan Co., 1943.

The Affirmation of Immortality. New York: The Macmillan Co., 1947.

My Gandhi. New York: Harper and Brothers, 1953.

I Speak for Myself. New York: Harper and Brothers, 1958.

The Collected Hymns of John Haynes Holmes. Boston: Beacon Press, 1960.

OTHER WRITINGS

Sermons bound in printed volumes of *The Messiah Pulpit* for the years 1907–1919 and *The Community Pulpit* for 1919–1949; occasional contributions to *The Community Pulpit* from 1950 to 1957.

Articles, sermons, and editorials from 1904 to 1964 in *Christian Register, Christian Leader, Christian Century, Survey, Survey Graphic, Century, North American Review, Atlantic, Nation, New Republic, Progressive, Newark Journal, Saturday Review, The Forum, Association Men* (YMCA), *The National Student,* etc.

Essays in the symposiums *My Idea of God: A Symposium of Faith,* edited by Joseph Fort Newton (Boston: Little, Brown & Co., 1926); *What I Owe to My Father,* edited by Sydney Strong, (New York: Henry Holt & Co., 1931); *The Beacon Song and Service Book* (Boston: Beacon Press, 1935); *Heralds of a Liberal Faith,* Vol. IV, *The Pilots,* edited by Samuel A. Eliot (Boston: Beacon Press, 1952); *Mysticism and the Modern Mind,* edited by Alfred P. Stiernotte (Indianapolis: Bobbs-Merrill Co., 1959); and others.

Writings as contributing editor of *The Unitarian* (1907–1910) and *The Unitarian Advance* (1910–1917); contributing editor of *The World Tomorrow* (1917–1934); contributing editor of *Unity* (1910–1919) and editor (1919–1945); contributing editor of *Opinion* (1931–1956); contributing editor of *Fellowship* (1943–1964).

Book reviews for many years in *Books* of the New York *Herald Tribune, The Evening Post Literary Review* and many other periodicals.

Introductions to *America Arraigned,* by Lucie Trent and R. Cheyney; *Youth and the Singing Shadows*, by B. D. Allinson; *The Social Evolution of Religion*, by George Willis Cooke; *Life of Jesus*, by Ernest Renan; *There Is a Psychic World*, by Horace Westwood; *Letters to a Disciple*, by Mohandas Gandhi; *The Personal Letters of Stephen Wise*, edited by Justine Wise Polier and James Waterman Wise; and many others.

INDEX

About the Editor

CARL HERMANN VOSS, clergyman, teacher, and author, was born and educated in Pittsburgh, Pennsylvania, receiving the degrees of Bachelor of Arts and Doctor of Philosophy at the University of Pittsburgh. He pursued graduate studies in Denmark and Switzerland, at Yale University and at the University of Chicago, and earned the Bachelor of Divinity degree at the Union Theological Seminary in New York City. Ordained as a minister in the United Church of Christ, he is also a member of the Unitarian Universalist Association; he has been pastor of churches in Raleigh, North Carolina, in Pittsburgh, and in Brooklyn and Saratoga Springs, New York. He has served as an executive of international church organizations in New York City and has taught at the New School for Social Research, Skidmore College, and the Theological School of St. Lawrence University. His other books include *Rabbi and Minister: The Friendship of Stephen S. Wise and John Haynes Holmes; Stephen S. Wise—Servant of the People: Selected Letters; The Universal God: The Eternal Quest in Which All Men Are Brothers; In Search of Meaning: Living Religions of the World;* and *The Palestine Problem Today: Israel and Its Neighbors.* He is editor of the Excalibur Books series. Dr. Voss and his wife, Phyllis Gierlotka Voss, live in Jacksonville, Florida, where Mrs. Voss is director of Bartram School, a college preparatory school for girls.